WRIGHT FAMILY
CENSUS, LAND GRANTS, LAND TAX, DEED, DEATH, AND PROBATE RECORDS

MONTGOMERY COUNTY, VIRGINIA

Robert N. Grant

HERITAGE BOOKS
2014

HERITAGE BOOKS

AN IMPRINT OF HERITAGE BOOKS, INC.

Books, CDs, and more—Worldwide

For our listing of thousands of titles see our website
at
www.HeritageBooks.com

Published 2014 by
HERITAGE BOOKS, INC.
Publishing Division
5810 Ruatan Street
Berwyn Heights, Md. 20740

International Standard Book Numbers
Paperbound: 978-0-7884-5535-3
Clothbound: 978-0-7884-9082-8

WRIGHT FAMILY

CENSUS RECORDS

1810 TO 1900

MONTGOMERY COUNTY, VIRGINIA

Revised as of December 27, 2010

This document is an appendix to a larger work titled Sorting Some Of The Wrights Of Southern Virginia. The work is divided into parts for each family of Wrights that has been researched. Each part is divided into two sections; the first section is text discussing the family and the evidence supporting the relationships and the second section is a descendants chart summarizing the relationships and information known about each individual.

The appendices to the work (of which this document is one) present source records for persons named Wright by county and by type of record with the identification of the person named and their Wright ancestors to the extent known.

The sources for the records listed in this appendix are the following:

1)   1810 Census, Montgomery County, Virginia, microfilm copy available at National Archives - Pacific Sierra Division, 1000 Commodore Drive, San Bruno, California 94066.

2)   1820 Census, Montgomery County, Virginia, microfilm copy available at the National Archives, Pacific Sierra Region, 1000 Commodore Drive, San Bruno, California 94066.

3)   1830 Census, Montgomery County, Virginia, microfilm copy available at the National Archives - Pacific Sierra Division, 1000 Commodore Drive, San Bruno, California 94066.

4)   1840 Census, Montgomery County, Virginia, microfilm copy available at the National Archives - Pacific Sierra Division, 1000 Commodore Drive, San Bruno, California 94066.

5)   1850 Census, Montgomery County, Virginia, microfilm copy available from the National Archives, Pacific Sierra Region, 1000 Commodore Drive, San Bruno, California 94066.

6)   Montgomery County, Va. Early Settlers 1810-1850 Census, transcribed by James L. Douthat, Mountain Press, P.O. Box 400, Signal Mountain, Tennessee 37377-0400, 1985.

7)   1860 Census, Montgomery County, Virginia, microfilm copy available at the Sutro Library, San Francisco, California, and at the National Archives, Pacific Sierra Region, 1000 Commodore Drive, San Bruno, California 94066.

8)   1870 Census Montgomery County, Virginia, microfilm copy available from the National Archives, Pacific Sierra Region, 1000 Commodore Drive, San Bruno, California 94066.

9)   1880 Census for Montgomery County, Virginia, microfilm copy available from the National Archives, Pacific Sierra Region, 1000 Commodore Drive, San Bruno, California 94066.

10) 1900 Census, Montgomery County, Virginia, available from Ancestry.com at http://www.ancestry.com.

The identification of a person or their ancestor by year and county indicates their year of death and county of residence at death. For example, "1763 Thomas Wright of Bedford County" indicates that this was the Thomas Wright who died in 1763 in Bedford County. If no state is listed after the county, the state is Virginia; counties in states other than Virginia will have a state listed after the county, as in "1876 William S. Wright of Highland County, Ohio".

A parenthetical after the name indicates an identification of the person when a place of death is not yet known, as in "John Wright (Goochland County Carpenter)". A county in parentheses after the name indicates the county with which that person was most identified when no evidence of the place of death has yet been found, as in "Grief Wright (Bedford County)".

All or portions of the text and descendants charts for each Wright family identified are available from the author:

Robert N. Grant
15 Campo Bello Court   (H) 650-854-0895
Menlo Park, California 94025   (O) 650-614-3800

This is a work in process and I would be most interested in receiving additional information about any of the persons identified in these records in order to correct any errors or expand on the information given.

1810 CENSUS

MONTGOMERY COUNTY, VIRGINIA

Appendix: Montgomery County, Virginia, 1810 Census:

Name of Town, city or County	Names of Heads of families	Free White Males					Free White Females				
		Under ten years of age to 10	Of ten years, and under sixteen to 16	Of sixteen, and under twenty-six including heads of families to 26	Of twenty-six and under forty-five includ-ing heads of families to 45	Of forty five and upwards, including heads of families 45&c	Under ten years of age to 10	Of ten years, and under sixteen to 16	Of sixteen, and under twenty-six including heads of families to 26	Of twenty-six and under forty five, in-cluding heads of families to 45	Of forty-five and upwards, including heads of families 45&c
	John Wright	3	2	1	0	1	2	1	1	0	1
	Jno Wright, Jr.	0	0	0	1	0	0	0	0	1	0

Appendix: Montgomery County, Virginia, 1810 Census:

Names of Heads of families [continued from prior page]	All other free persons except Indians, not taxed	Slaves	Identification
John Wright	0	0	John Wright (Montgomery County), son of 1815 Joseph Wright of Bedford County and grandson of 1763 Thomas Wright of Bedford County
Jno Wright, Jr.	0	0	John Wright, probably son of John Wright (Montgomery County), grandson of 1815 Joseph Wright of Bedford County, and great grandson of 1763 Thomas Wright of Bedford County

1820 CENSUS

MONTGOMERY COUNTY, VIRGINIA

Appendix: Montgomery County, Virginia, 1820 Census:

	Names of Heads of Families	Free White Males						Free White Females				
		Free white males under ten years to 10	Free white males of ten and under sixteen to 16	Free white males between sixteen and eighteen 16 to 18	Free white males of sixteen and under twenty-six including heads of families 16 to 26	Free white males of twenty-six and under forty-five, including heads of families to 45	Free white males of forty-five and upwards, including heads of families 45, &c.	Free white females under ten years of age to 10	Free white females of ten and under sixteen to 16	Free white females of six-teen and under twenty-six, including heads of families to 26	Free white females of twenty-six and under forty-five, including heads of families to 45	Free white females of forty-five, and upwards including heads of families 45, &c.
Mont Cty	John Wright	0	3	0	0	0	1	0	0	2	0	1
Mont Cty	Sir Francis G. Wright	0	0	0	1	0	0	1	0	1	0	0
Mont Cty	George Wright	1	2	0	0	0	1	1	1	1	1	0
Blacksbrg	Reed Wright	0	1	0	1	0	1	4	2	0	1	0
Mont Cty	David Wright	2	1	1	1	0	1	2	2	0	0	1
Mont Cty	Samuel Wright	1	2	0	0	1	0	2	2	0	1	0
Mont Cty	Joseph Wright	0	0	0	1	0	0	1	0	1	0	0

Appendix: Montgomery County, Virginia, 1820 Census:

Names of Heads of Families [continued from prior page]	Foreigners not natur-alized	Number of persons engaged in Agriculture	Number of persons engaged in Commerce	Number of persons engaged in Manu-facture	Slaves							
					Males				Females			
					Males under fourteen to 14	Males of fourteen and under twenty-six to 26	Males of twenty-six and under forty-five to 45	Males of forty-five and upwards 45, &c.	Females of (under) fourteen to 14	Females of fourteen and under twenty-six to 26	Females of twenty-six and under forty-five to 45	Females of forty-five and upwards 45, &c.
John Wright	0	2										
Sir Francis G. Wright	0	1										
George Wright	0	2										
Reed Wright	0	2										
David Wright	0	2										
Samuel Wright	0	2										
Joseph Wright	0	1										

Appendix: Montgomery County, Virginia, 1820 Census:

| Names of Heads of Families [continued from prior page] | Free Colored Persons | | | | | | | | | Identification |
| | Males | | | | Females | | | | All other persons except Indians not taxed | |
	Males under fourteen years to 14	Males of fourteen and under twenty-six to 26	Males of twenty-six and under forty-five to 45	Males of forty five and upwards 45, &c	Females under fourteen years to 14	Females of fourteen and under twenty-six to 26	Females of twenty-six and under forty-five to 45	Females of forty-five and upwards 45, &c		
John Wright										John Wright (Montgomery County), son of 1815 Joseph Wright of Bedford County and grandson of 1763 Thomas Wright of Bedford County
Sir Francis G. Wright										Surfrancis G. or D. Wright, probably son of John Wright (Montgomery County, grandson of 1815 Joseph Wright of Bedford County, and great grandson of 1763 Thomas Wright of Bedford County
George Wright										
Reed Wright										
David Wright										
Samuel Wright										
Joseph Wright										1856 Joseph Wright of Roanoke County, son of John Wright (Montgomery County), grandson of 1815 Joseph Wright of Bedford County, and great grandson of 1763 Thomas Wright of Bedford County

Appendix: Montgomery County, Virginia, 1820 Census:

	Names of Heads of Families	Free White Males						Free White Females				
		Free white males under ten years to 10	Free white males of ten and under sixteen to 16	Free white males between sixteen and eighteen 16 to 18	Free white males of sixteen and under twenty-six including heads of families 16 to 26	Free white males of twenty-six and under forty-five, including heads of families to 45	Free white males of forty- five and upwards, including heads of families 45, &c.	Free white females under ten years of age to 10	Free white females of ten and under sixteen to 16	Free white females of six-teen and under twenty-six, including heads of families to 26	Free white females of twenty-six and under forty-five, including heads of families to 45	Free white females of forty-five, and upwards including heads of families 45, &c.
Mont Cty	Richard Wright	1	0	0	0	1	0	1	1	0	1	0
Mont Cty	John Wright Sr.	0	0	0	0	0	1	0	1	0	0	1
Mont Cty	John Wright Jr.	3	0	0	0	1	0	2	0	0	1	0
Mont Cty	Charles Wright	2	0	0	0	1	0	1	0	0	1	0

Appendix: Montgomery County, Virginia, 1820 Census:

Names of Heads of Families [continued from prior page]	Foreigners not natur- alized	Number of persons engaged in Agriculture	Number of persons engaged in Commerce	Number of persons engaged in Manu- facture	Slaves							
					Males				Females			
					Males under fourteen to 14	Males of fourteen and under twenty-six to 26	Males of twenty-six and under forty-five to 45	Males of forty-five and upwards 45, &c.	Females of (under) fourteen to 14	Females of fourteen and under twenty-six to 26	Females of twenty-six and under forty-five to 45	Females of forty- five and upwards 45, &c.
Richard Wright	0	1										
John Wright Sr.	0	1										
John Wright Jr.	0	1										
Charles Wright	0	1										

Appendix: Montgomery County, Virginia, 1820 Census:

	Free Colored Persons									
	Males				Females					
Names of Heads of Families [continued from prior page]	Males under fourteen years to 14	Males of fourteen and under twenty-six to 26	Males of twenty-six and under forty-five to 45	Males of forty five and upwards 45, &c	Females under fourteen years to 14	Females of fourteen and under twenty-six to 26	Females of twenty-six and under forty-five to 45	Females of forty-five and upwards 45, &c	All other persons except Indians not taxed	Identification
Richard Wright										
John Wright Sr.										John Wright, Sr. (Russell County)
John Wright Jr.										John Wright, Jr. (Wise County), son of John Wright, Sr. (Russell County)
Charles Wright										

1830 CENSUS

MONTGOMERY COUNTY, VIRGINIA

| Names Heads of Families | Free White Persons (including heads of families) Males | | | | | | | | | | | | |
	Under five years of age under 5	Of five and under ten 5 to 10	Of ten and under fifteen 10 to 15	Of fifteen and under twenty 15 to 20	Of twenty and under thirty 20 to 30	Of thirty and under forty 30 to 40	Of forty and under fifty 40 to 50	Of fifty and under sixty 50 to 60	Of sixty and under seventy 60 to 70	Of seventy and under eighty 70 to 80	Of eighty and under ninety 80 to 90	Of ninety and under one hundred 90 to 100	Of one hundred and upwards 100, &c.
John Wright	0	0	0	0	2	0	0	0	1	0	0	0	0
Francis Wright	2	2	0	0	0	1	0	0	0	0	0	0	0
Smith Wright	1	1	1	0	0	1	0	0	0	0	0	0	0

Appendix: Montgomery County, Virginia, 1830 Census

| Names Heads of Families | Free White Persons (including heads of families) [Continued] | | | | | | | | | | | | |
| | Females | | | | | | | | | | | | |
	Under five years of age under 5	Of five and under ten 5 to 10	Of ten and under fifteen 10 to 15	Of fifteen and under twenty 15 to 20	Of twenty and under thirty 20 to 30	Of thirty and under forty 30 to 40	Of forty and under fifty 40 to 50	Of fifty and under sixty 50 to 60	Of sixty and under seventy 60 to 70	Of seventy and under eighty 70 to 80	Of eighty and under ninety 80 to 90	Of ninety and under one hundred 90 to 100	Of one hundred and upwards 100, &c.
John Wright	1	0	0	0	1	0	0	0	1	0	0	0	0
Francis Wright		1	0	0	1	0	0	0	0	0	0	0	0
Smith Wright	1	0	2	0	0	1	0	0	0	0	0	0	0

Appendix: Montgomery County, Virginia, 1830 Census

| | Slaves | | | | | | | | | | | |
| | Males | | | | | | Females | | | | | |
Names Heads of Families [Continued from prior page]	Under ten years of age under 10	Of ten and under twenty-four 10 to 24	Of twenty- four and under thirty-six 24 to 36	Of thirty- six and under fifty-five 36 to 55	Of fifty- five and under one hundred 55 to 100	Of one hundred and upwards 100, &c	Under ten years of age under 10	Of ten and under twenty-four 10 to 24	Of twenty- four and under thirty-six 24 to 36	Of thirty- six and under fifty-five 36 to 55	Of fifty- five and under one hundred 55 to 100	Of one hundred and upwards 100, &c
John Wright												
Francis Wright												
Smith Wright												

Appendix: Montgomery County, Virginia, 1830 Census

	Free Colored Persons											
	Males						Females					
Names Heads of Families [Continued from prior page]	Under ten years of age under 10	Of ten and under twenty-four 10 to 24	Of twenty-four and under thirty-six 24 to 36	Of thirty-six and under fifty-five 36 to 55	Of fifty-five and under one hundred 55 to 100	Of one hundred and upwards 100, &c	Under ten years of age under 10	Of ten and under twenty-four 10 to 24	Of twenty-four and under thirty-six 24 to 36	Of thirty-six and under fifty-five 36 to 55	Of fifty-five and under one hundred 55 to 100	Of one hundred and upwards 100, &c
John Wright												
Francis Wright												
Smith Wright												

Names Heads of Families [Continued from prior page]	Total	White Persons included in the foregoing					Slaves and Colored Persons, included in the foregoing				Identification
		Who are Deaf and Dumb, under fourteen years of age under 14	Who are Deaf and Dumb, of the age of fourteen and under twenty-five 14 to 25	Who are Deaf and Dumb, of twenty-five and upwards 25, &c.	Who are blind	Aliens - Foreigners and naturalized	Who are Deaf and Dumb, under fourteen years of age under 14	Who are Deaf and Dumb, of the age of fourteen and under twenty-five 14-25	Who are Deaf and Dumb of twenty-five and upwards 25, &c.	Who are blind	
John Wright	6										John Wright (Montgomery County), son of 1815 Joseph Wright of Bedford County and grandson of 1763 Thomas Wright of Bedford County
Francis Wright	7										Surfrancis G. or D. Wright, probably son of John Wright (Montgomery County), grandson of 1815 Joseph Wright of Bedford County, and great grandson of 1763 Thomas Wright of Bedford County
Smith Wright	8										Smith Wright (Montgomery County), probably son of John Wright (Montgomery County), grandson of 1815 Joseph Wright of Bedford County, and great grandson of 1763 Thomas Wright of Bedford County

1840 CENSUS

MONTGOMERY COUNTY, VIRGINIA

Names of Heads of Families	Free White Persons (including heads of families) Females												
	Under 5	5 & under 10	10 & under 15	15 & under 20	20 & under 30	30 & under 40	40 & under 50	50 & under 60	60 & under 70	70 & under 80	80 & under 90	90 & under 100	100 and upwards
Amos Wright	0	0	0	0	0	1	0	0	0	0	0	0	0
Alexander Wright	2	0	0	0	1	0	0	0	0	0	0	0	0

Appendix: Montgomery County, Virginia, 1840 Census

Names of Heads of Families	Free White Persons (including heads of families)												
	Males												
	Under 5	5 & under 10	10 & under 15	15 & under 20	20 & under 30	30 & under 40	40 & under 50	50 & under 60	60 & under 70	70 & under 80	80 & under 90	90 & under 100	100 and upwards
Amos Wright	0	0	0	1	1	0	0	0	0	0	0	0	0
Alexander Wright	0	0	0	0	1	0	0	0	0	0	0	0	0

Names of Heads of Families [Continued from prior page]	Free Colored Persons											
	Males						Females					
	Under 10	10 & under 24	24 & under 36	36 & under 55	55 & under 100	100 & and upwards	5 & under 10	10 & under 24	24 & under 36	36 & under 55	55 & under 100	100 and upwards
Amos Wright												
Alexander Wright												

Appendix: Montgomery County, Virginia, 1840 Census

Names of Heads of Families [Continued from prior page]	Slaves												Total
	Males						Females						
	Under 10	10 & under 24	24 & under 36	36 & under 55	55 & under 100	100 and upwards	Under 10	10 & under 24	24 & under 36	36 & under 55	55 & under 100	100 and upwards	
Amos Wright													3
Alexander Wright													4

Names of Heads of Families [Continued from prior page]	Number of Persons in each Family Employed in							Pensioners for Revolutionary or Military Services Included in the foregoing Names		Deaf and Dumb, Blind and Insane White Persons Included in the Foregoing					
										Deaf and Dumb				Insane and Idiots	
	Mining	Agri-culture	Commerce	Manu-facture and trades	Navi-gation of the ocean	Navi-gation of canals lakes and rivers	Learned profes-sions and engineers	Names	Ages	Under 14	14 & under 25	25 and upwards	Blind	Insane and idiots at public charge	Insane and idiots at private charge
Amos Wright		1													
Alexander Wright		1													

Appendix: Montgomery County, Virginia, 1840 Census

Names of Heads of Families [Continued from prior page]	Deaf and Dumb, Blind and Insane Colored Persons Included in the Foregoing				Schools, &c.							
	Deaf, Dumb, and Blind		Insane and Idiots									
	Deaf & Dumb	Blind	Insane and idiots at private charge	Insane and idiots at public charge	Univer-sities or College	Number of Students	Academies & Grammar Schools	No. of Scholars	Primary and Common Schools	No. of Scholars	No. of Scholars at public charge
Amos Wright											
Alexander Wright											

Appendix: Montgomery County, Virginia, 1840 Census

Names of Heads of Families [Continued from prior page]	No. of white persons over 90 years of age in each family who cannot read or write	Identification
Amos Wright		Amos Wright, son of Sarah Wright and grandson of 1826 Joseph Wright of Augusta County
Alexander Wright		

1850 CENSUS

MONTGOMERY COUNTY, VIRGINIA

Appendix: Montgomery County, Virginia, 1850 Census

Name	Age	Sex	Color	Occupation	Value of Real Estate	Place of Birth	Married Within Year	Attended School Within Year	Cannot Read & Write	Deaf Dumb Blind Insane etc.	Identification
618/618 09/05/1850											
James M. Dobbins	28	M				Virginia					
Ann Wright	25	F				Virginia					
938/938 11/18/1850											
Amos Wright	49	M		Farmer	$1500	Virginia					Amos Wright, son of Sarah Wright and grandson of 1826 Joseph Wright of Augusta County
Levinia Wright	40	F				Virginia					
William Wright	8	M				Virginia					
Virginia Wright	4	F				Virginia					
Sarah Wright	71	F				Virginia					

1860 CENSUS

MONTGOMERY COUNTY, VIRGINIA

Name	Age	Sex	Color	Occupation	Value of Real Estate	Value of Personal Property	Place of Birth	Married Within Year	Attended School Within Year	Cannot Read & Write	Deaf Dumb Blind Insane etc.	Identification

Lafayette & Shawsville P.O.
317/302 07/06/1860

Name	Age	Sex	Color	Occupation	Value of Real Estate	Value of Personal Property	Place of Birth	Married Within Year	Attended School Within Year	Cannot Read & Write	Deaf Dumb Blind Insane etc.	Identification
Walter C Deyerle	43	M	X	Distiller	2300	6500	Virginia					William F. Wright, son of
William F Wright	23	M	X	Cooper			Virginia					James A. Wright (Floyd County),
John F Murray	22	M	X	Laborer			Virginia					grandson of Joseph Wright
Micajah Myers	21	M	X	Laborer			Virginia					(Augusta County), and great grandson of 1826 Joseph Wright of Augusta County

Christiansburg P.O.
461/434 07/19/1860

Name	Age	Sex	Color	Occupation	Value of Real Estate	Value of Personal Property	Place of Birth	Married Within Year	Attended School Within Year	Cannot Read & Write	Deaf Dumb Blind Insane etc.	Identification
Amos Wright	57	M	X	Farmer	2500	375	Virginia					Amos Wright, son of Sarah
Lavinia Wright	49	F					Virginia					Wright and godson of 1826
William Wright	17	M	X	Farmer			Virginia		1			Joseph Wright of Augusta
Virginia Wright	13	F					Virginia					County

Christiansburg & Shawsville P.O.
1557/1437 11/05/1860

Name	Age	Sex	Color	Occupation	Value of Real Estate	Value of Personal Property	Place of Birth	Married Within Year	Attended School Within Year	Cannot Read & Write	Deaf Dumb Blind Insane etc.	Identification
Samuel A McCondley	37	M	X	Physician	12000	7000	Virginia					Theodrick or Theodore F.
Theodore F Wright	22	M	X	Trader	2000	10000	Virginia					Wright, son of 1845 William
John Rock	32	M	X	Distiller	1200		Virginia					Wright of Franklin County, grandson of 1830 William Wright of Franklin County, great grandson of 1809 William Wright of Frankllin County, great great grandson of 1792 John Wright of Farquier County, and possibly great great great grandson of John Wright (Westmoreland County Overseer)

Appendix: Montgomery County, Virginia, 1860 Census

Name	Age	Sex	Color	Occupation	Value of Real Estate	Value of Personal Property	Place of Birth	Married Within Year	Attended School Within Year	Cannot Read & Write	Deaf Dumb Blind Insane etc.	Identification
Montgomery County, Virginia 1377/1263 10/16 & 17/1860												
Joseph Miller	48	M		Farmer	2950	350	Virginia					
Elizabeth Miller	47	F					Virginia			R		
John T Miller	22	M		Farmer			Virginia					
George W Miller	20	M					Virginia					
Edward J Miller	18	M					Virginia					
Harriet V Miller	16	F					Virginia					
Giles P Miller	14	M					Virginia					
Joseph C Miller	12	M					Virginia					
Frances E Miller	6	F					Virginia					
William C Miller	4	M					Virginia					
Jonathan T Miller	2	M					Virginia					
Nancy Wright	27	F					Virginia					

32.

1870 CENSUS

MONTGOMERY COUNTY, VIRGINIA

Name	Age	Sex	Color	Occupation	Value of Real Estate	Value of Personal Property	Place of Birth	Married Within Year	Born Within Year	Attended School Within Year	Cannot Read	Cannot Write	Deaf Dumb Blind Insane or or Idiot
288/297 09/23/1870													
Ewing A Wright	43	M	W	Farmer	500	400	Virginia						
Julia Wright	35	F	W	Keeping House			Virginia				1	1	
Edward M Wright	25	M	W	Works on Farm			Virginia				1	1	
Mark S Wright	12	M	W	Works on Farm			Virginia				1	1	
John B Wright	11	M	W	Works on Farm			Virginia				1	1	
Gordon R Wright	9	M	W	at Home			Virginia						
William C Wright	7	M	W	at Home			Virginia						
Naoma L Wright	5	F	W	at Home			Virginia						
Harriet Wright	2	F	W	at Home			Virginia						
Mary M Wright	11/12	F	W	at Home			Virginia		Feb				
001/001 09/18/1870													
Columbus H Wright	37	M	W	Blacksmith			Virginia				1	1	
Medora J Wright	21	F	W	Keeping House			Virginia						
Virginia A Wright	12	F	W	at Home			Virginia				1	1	
James H Wright	7	M	W				Virginia						
Lennis Wright	4	F	W				Virginia						
Eliza A Wright	1	F	W				Virginia						
007/007 09/18/1870													
Elizabeth Wright	38	F	W	Keeping House			Virginia				1	1	
Lucy Wright	15	F	W	At Home			Virginia				1	1	
Elizabeth Webb	46	F	W	Keeping House			Virginia						
Sarena Webb	14	F	W	At Home			Virginia					1	
Sarah Webb	12	F	W				Virginia				1	1	
Jacob Gillispie	2	M	W				Virginia						

Appendix: Montgomery County, Virginia, 1870 Census

Name [Continued from prior page]	Male Citizen Over 21	Male Citizen Over 21 Without Right to Vote	Identification
288/297 09/23/1870			
Ewing A Wright Julia Wright Edward M Wright Mark S Wright John B Wright Gordon R Wright William C Wright Naoma L Wright Harriet Wright Mary M Wright	1		Ewing A. Wright, son of 1856 Joseph Wright of Roanoke County, grandson of John Wright (Montgomery County), great grandson of 1815 Joseph Wright of Bedford Coiunty, and great great grandson of 1763 Thomas Wright of Bedford County
001/001 09/18/1870			
Columbus H Wright Medora J Wright Virginia A Wright James H Wright Lennis Wright Eliza A Wright	1		Columbus H. Wright, son of Robert B. Wright, grandson of 1815 Robert C. Wright of Prince Edward County, great grandson of Pryor Wright, Sr., of Prince Edward County, and great great grandson of 1779 John Wright of Prince Edward County
007/007 09/18/1870			
Elizabeth Wright Lucy Wright Elizabeth Webb Sarena Webb Sarah Webb Jacob Gillispie			

Appendix: Montgomery County, Virginia, 1870 Census

Name	Age	Sex	Color	Occupation	Value of Real Estate	Value of Personal Property	Place of Birth	Married Within Year	Born Within Year	Attended School Within Year	Cannot Read	Cannot Write	Deaf Dumb Blind Insane or Idiot
020/022 09/30/1870													
Calvin Wright	43	M	B	Farm Laborer			Virginia				1	1	
Harriet Wright	42	F	B	Keeping House			Virginia				1	1	
Catharine Wright	16	F	B	House Work			Virginia				1	1	
Mary A Wright	14	F	B	House Work			Virginia				1	1	
Abram Wright	13	M	B				Virginia						
023/025 09/30/1870													
William Cole	96	M	B	Decepid			Virginia				1	1	
Mary Wright	83	F	B				Virginia						
016/016 07/13/1870													
John M Wright	33	M	W	Farmer	500	500	Virginia						
Elmira Wright	28	F	W	Keeping House			Virginia					1	
Mary Howry	81	F	W	House Keeper			Virginia					1	
Thomas Luster	12	M	W	Works on Farm			Virginia					1	
Kelly Jefferson	10	M	W				Virginia				1	1	
059/062 07/13/1870													
Nathaniel Wright	45	M	B	Farm Laborer			Virginia				1	1	
Alexis Wright	25	F	B	Keeping House			Virginia				1	1	
Mathew Wright	11	M	B	Works on Farm			Virginia				1	1	
Andrew Wright	7	M	B				Virginia						
Phoebe Wright	3	F	B				Virginia						
Biddy Wright	6/12	F	B				Virginia		Jan				No
Peggy Wright	60	F	B				Virginia				1	1	
Leonora Johnson	5	F	B				Virginia						

Appendix: Montgomery County, Virginia, 1870 Census

Name [Continued from prior page]	Male Citizen Over 21	Male Citizen Over 21 Without Right to Vote	Identification
020/022 09/30/1870			
Calvin Wright	1		Calvin Wright, son of Henry Wright
Harriet Wright			
Catharine Wright			
Mary A Wright			
Abram Wright			
023/025 09/30/1870			
William Cole	1		
Mary Wright			
016/016 07/13/1870			
John M Wright	1		1902 John M. Wright of Montgomery County, son of James A. Wright (Floyd County), grandson of Joseph Wright (Augusta County), and great grandson of 1826 Joseph Wright of Augusta County
Elmira Wright			
Mary Howry			
Thomas Luster			
Kelly Jefferson			
059/062 07/13/1870			
Nathaniel Wright	1		
Alexis Wright			
Mathew Wright			
Andrew Wright			
Phoebe Wright			
Biddy Wright			
Peggy Wright			
Leonora Johnson			

Name	Age	Sex	Color	Occupation	Value of Real Estate	Value of Personal Property	Place of Birth	Married Within Year	Born Within Year	Attended School Within Year	Cannot Read	Cannot Write	Deaf Dumb Blind Insane or or Idiot
060/063 07/13/1870													
Allen Wright	40	M	B	Farm Laborer			Virginia				1	1	
Nancy Wright	25	F	B	Keeping House			Virginia				1	1	
Peggy Wright	13	F	B	at Home			Virginia				1	1	
Lewis Wright	8	M	B				Virginia						
Harriet Wright	6	F	B				Virginia						
Charlotte Wright	1	F	B				Virginia						
076/080 07/16/1870													
Stephen Childress	50	M	W	Farmer	15180(?)	1000	Virginia						
Sophia Childress	52	F	W	Keeping House			Virginia						
Charles T(?) Childress	22	M	W	Miller			Virginia						
Emily J Childress	19	F	W	at home			Virginia						
Joseph A Childress	18	M	W	Works on Farm			Virginia						
Henry H Childress	16	M	W	Works on Farm			Virginia						
Ann E Childress	12	F	W	at home			Virginia						
Mary S Childress	10	F	W				Virginia						
Benjamin F Childress	8	M	W				Virginia						
Louisa Wright	12	F	W	House Servant			Virginia						No
214/224 07/17/1870													
John B Lucas	28	M	W	Works on Farm			Virginia						
L_ Lucas	26	F	W	Keeping House			Virginia						
William S Lucas	1	M	W				Virginia						
George C Surface(?)	9	M	W				Virginia						
Thomas Wright	19	M	B	Farm Laborer			Virginia				1	1	

Appendix: Montgomery County, Virginia, 1870 Census

Name [Continued from prior page]	Male Citizen Over 21	Male Citizen Over 21 Without Right to Vote	Identification
060/063 07/13/1870			
Allen Wright	1		
Nancy Wright			
Peggy Wright			
Lewis Wright			
Harriet Wright			
Charlotte Wright			
076/080 07/16/1870			
Stephen Childress	1		
Sophia Childress			
Charles T(?) Childress			
Emily J Childress			
Joseph A Childress			
Henry H Childress			
Ann E Childress			
Mary S Childress			
Benjamin F Childress			
Louisa Wright			
214/224 07/17/1870			
John B Lucas	1		
L__ Lucas			
William S Lucas			
George Surface(?)			
Thomas Wright			

Name	Age	Sex	Color	Occupation	Value of Real Estate	Value of Personal Property	Place of Birth	Married Within Year	Born Within Year	Attended School Within Year	Cannot Read	Cannot Write	Deaf Dumb Blind Insane or or Idiot
408/403 08/13/1870													
Ferdinand Wright	35	M	B				Virginia				1	1	
Martha Wright	30	F	B	Keeping House	100		Virginia				1	1	
James Wright	14	M	B	Works on Farm			Virginia				1	1	
Mary Wright	10	F	B	at Home			Virginia				1	1	
Reubin Wright	8	M	B				Virginia						
Emily Wright	6	F	B				Virginia						
Frances B Wright	4	F	B				Virginia						
Judith Wright	1	F	B				Virginia						
523/547 09/19/1870													
Daniel Wright	29	M	B	Farm Laborer			Virginia						
Elizabeth Wright	25	F	B	House Work			Virginia						
Louisa Wright	2	F	B	At Home			Virginia						
Wheeler T Wright	1	M	B				Virginia						
575/601 09/24/1870													
Alsop Wright	52	M	W	Blacksmith		125	Virginia						
Elizabeth Wright	36	F	W	Keeping House			Virginia						
Mary A Wright	21	F	W	At Home			Virginia						
John H Wright	16	M	W	Day Laborer			Virginia						
Samuel L Wright	13	M	W	At Home			Virginia				1	1	
Nanney(?) C Wright	11	F	W	At Home			Virginia						
Martin J Wright	6	M	W	At Home			Virginia						
Thomas L Wright	1	M	W				Virginia						

Appendix: Montgomery County, Virginia, 1870 Census

Name [Continued from prior page]	Male Citizen Over 21	Male Citizen Over 21 Without Right to Vote	Identification
408/403 08/13/1870			
Ferdinand Wright	1		Ferdinand Wright, son of George Wright
Martha Wright			
James Wright			
Mary Wright			
Reubin Wright			
Emily Wright			
Frances B Wright			
Judith Wright			
523/547 09/19/1870			
Daniel Wright	1		Daniel Wright, son of Harry Wright
Elizabeth Wright			
Louisa Wright			
Wheeler T Wright			
575/601 09/24/1870			
Alsop Wright	1		Alsup or Alsop Wright, son of Grief Wright (Bedford County)
Elizabeth Wright			
Mary A Wright			
John H Wright			
Samuel L Wright			
Nanney(?) C Wright			
Martin J Wright			
Thomas L Wright			

Name	Age	Sex	Color	Occupation	Value of Real Estate	Value of Personal Property	Place of Birth	Married Within Year	Born Within Year	Attended School Within Year	Cannot Read	Cannot Write	Deaf Dumb Blind Insane or or Idiot
087/104 06/16/1870													
Joseph D Feather	41	M	W	Blacksmith	1500	1000	Virginia						
Abagil Feather	42	F	W	Keeping House			Virginia						
Mary A Feather	15	F	W				Virginia			1			
Susan P Feather	13	F	W				Virginia			1			
Louan V Feather	10	F	W				Virginia			1			
John C Feather	5	M	W				Virginia						
Ada Feather	3	F	W				Virginia						
James M Wright	19	M	W	Blacksmith apprentice			Virginia						
244/277 06/25/1870													
Caroline Wiginton	30	F	W	Keeping House			Virginia						
Catharine Wiginton	12	F	W				Virginia						
Robert Wiginton	10	M	W				Virginia				1	1	
Samuel Wiginton	8	M	W				Virginia						
Millie Wiginton	1/12	F	W				Virginia						
William Wright	29	M	W	Farmer			Virginia				1	1	
383/424 07/04/1870													
Samuel C Shelton	27	M	W	Carpenter		250	Virginia						
Nancy C Shelton	32	F	W	Keeping House			Virginia						
William Shelton	12	M	W				Virginia						
James Shelton	8	M	W				Virginia						
Samuel Shelton	6	M	W				Virginia						No
Charles H Shelton	4	M	W				Virginia						
Robert L Shelton	1	M	W				Virginia						
Amoss Wright	68	M	W	Farm Laborer			Virginia						No
Lavinia Wright	57	F	W	House Keeper			Virginia						
Catharine Fysor	8	F	W				Virginia						

Appendix: Montgomery County, Virginia, 1870 Census

Name [Continued from prior page]	Male Citizen Over 21	Male Citizen Over 21 Without Right to Vote	Identification
087/104 06/16/1870			
Joseph D Feather	1		
Abagil Feather			
Mary A Feather			
Susan P Feather			
Louan V Feather			
John C Feather			
Ada Feather			
James M Wright			
244/277 06/25/1870			
Caroline Wiginton			Possibly William Wright, son of Amos Wright, grandson of Sarah Wright, and great grandson of 1826 Joseph Wright of Augusta County
Catharine Wiginton			
Robert Wiginton			
Samuel Wiginton			
Millie Wiginton			
William Wright	1		
383/424 07/04/1870			
Samuel C Shelton	1		Amos Wright, son of Sarah Wright and grandson of 1826 Joseph Wright of Augusta County
Nancy C Shelton			
William Shelton			
James Shelton			
Samuel Shelton			
Charles H Shelton			
Robert L Shelton			
Amoss Wright	1		
Lavinia Wright			
Catharine Fysor			

1880 CENSUS

MONTGOMERY COUNTY, VIRGINIA

Name	Color	Sex	Age	Month of Birth	Relationship	Marital Status	Married During Year	Occupation	Months Unem-ployed	Sickness Blind Deaf & Dumb Idiotic Disabled
49th Enumeration District **19th day of June, 1880**										
Dwelling #333/Family #340										
Amos Wright	W	M	78			M				Rheumatism
Lavinia Wright	W	F	78		Wife	M		Keeping House		
Dwelling #367/Family #377										
Daniel Wright	B	M	43			W/D		Laborer		
Martha Taylor	B	F	38		Servant	S		House Keeping		
June 22, 1880										
Dwelling #303/Family #340										
Allsup Wright	W	M	60			M		Farmer		
Harriett Wright	W	F	44		Wife	M		Keeping House		
Martin J Wright	W	M	18		Son	S		Farm Hand		
Nicholis H Wright	W	M	7		Son	S		at Home		
Edward B Wright	W	M	4		Son	S		at Home		
Nancy C Wright	W	F	19		Daughter	S				
Hattie B Wright	W	F	2		Daughter	S				
Dwelling #306/Family #343										
Samuel Wright	W	M	23			M		L Farmer		
Maggie J Wright	W	F	18		Wife	M		Keeps house		
Janus A Wright	W	M	1		Daughter	S				

Appendix: Montgomery County, Virginia, 1880 Census

Name continued from previous page]	Attended School Within Year	Cannot Read	Cannot Write	Born	Father Born	Mother Born	Identification
49th Enumeration District 19th day of June, 1880							
Dwelling #333/Family #340							
Amos Wright				Virginia	Va	Va	Amos Wright, son of Sarah Wright and grandson of 1826 Joseph
Lavinia Wright				Virginia	Va	Va	Wright of Augusta County
Dwelling #367/Family #377							
Daniel Wright				Virginia	Va	Va	Daniel Wright, son of Harry Wright
Martha Taylor				Virginia	Va	Va	
June 22, 1880							
Dwelling #303/Family #340							
Allsup Wright			1	Va	Va	Va	Alsup Wright, son of Grief Wright (Bedford County)
Harriett Wright				Va	Va	Va	
Martin J Wright				Va	Va	Va	
Nicholis H Wright				Va	Va	Va	
Edward B Wright				Va	Va	Va	
Nancy C Wright				Va	Va	Va	
Hattie B Wright				Va	Va	Va	
Dwelling #316/Family #343							
Samuel Wright				Va	Va	Va	Samuel L. Wright, son of Alsup Wright and grandson of Grief
Maggie J Wright				Va	Va	Va	Wright (Bedford County)
Janus A Wright				Va	Va	Va	

Name	Color	Sex	Age	Month of Birth	Relationship	Marital Status	Married During Year	Occupation	Months Unemployed	Sickness Blind Deaf & Dumb Idiotic Disabled

Allegheny District
4 day of June, 1880

Dwelling #60/Family #62

Name	Color	Sex	Age	Month of Birth	Relationship	Marital Status	Married During Year	Occupation	Months Unemployed	Sickness Blind Deaf & Dumb Idiotic Disabled
Calvin Wright	B	M	57			M		Workes on farm		
Harriet Wright	B	F	44		Wife	M		Keeping house		
Luther Wright	Mu	M	7		Gran Son	S				
Harriett R Wright	Mu	F	4		Gran Daughter	S				
Agnes Wright	B	M	5		Gran Daughter	S				

Dwelling #345/Family #350

Name	Color	Sex	Age	Month of Birth	Relationship	Marital Status	Married During Year	Occupation	Months Unemployed	Sickness Blind Deaf & Dumb Idiotic Disabled
Jackson Wright	B	M	26			M		Workes on farm		
Margret Wright	B	F	23		Wife	M		Keeping house		
John W Wright	B	M	3		Son	S				
Fannie Wright	B	F	8/12	Oct	Daughter	S				
Mollie Whitlock	B	F	13		Niece	S		Cooks		

55th Enumeration District
June 16, 1880

Dwelling #200/Family #200

Name	Color	Sex	Age	Month of Birth	Relationship	Marital Status	Married During Year	Occupation	Months Unemployed	Sickness Blind Deaf & Dumb Idiotic Disabled
Ferdinand Wright	B	M	76			M		Farmer		
Eliza Wright	B	F	21		Wife	M				
Mary Wright	B	F	18		Daughter	S				
Emily Wright	B	F	16		Daughter	S				
Belle Wright	B	F	14		Daughter	S				
Julia Wright	B	F	10		Daughter	S				

Appendix: Montgomery County, Virginia, 1880 Census

Name continued from previous page]	Attended School Within Year	Cannot Read	Cannot Write	Born	Father Born	Mother Born	Identification
Allegheny District 4 day of June, 1880							
Dwelling #60/Family #62							
Calvin Wright		1	1	Virginia	Va	Va	Calvin Wright, son of Harry Wright
Harriet Wright		1	1	Virginia	Va	Va	
Luther Wright		X	X	Virginia	Va	Va	
Harriett R Wrigh		X	X	Virginia	Va	Va	
Agnes Wright		X	X	Virginia	Va	Va	
Dwelling #345/Family #350							
Jackson Wright		1	1	Virginia	Va	Va	Jackson Wright, son of Calvin Wright and grandson of Harry
Margret Wright		1	1	Virginia	Va	Va	Wright
John W Wright				Virginia	Va	Va	
Fannie Wright				Virginia	Va	Va	
Mollie Whitlock		1	1	Virginia	Va	Va	
55th Enumeration District June 16, 1880							
Dwelling #200/Family #200							
Ferdinand Wright		1	1	Virginia	Va	Va	Ferdinand Wright, son of George Wright
Eliza Wright		1	1	Virginia	Va	Va	
Mary Wright	1			Virginia	Va	Va	
Emily Wright	1		1	Virginia	Va	Va	
Belle Wright		1	1	Virginia	Va	Va	
Julia Wright		1	1	Virginia	Va	Va	

Name	Color	Sex	Age	Month of Birth	Relationship	Marital Status	Married During Year	Occupation	Months Unemployed	Sickness Blind Deaf & Dumb Idiotic Disabled
56th Enumeration Dist										
10th day of June, 1880										
Dwelling #149/Family #184										
Nathaniel Wright	B	M	58			M		Farmer		1
Elsey Wright	Mu	F	38		wife	M		Keeping House		
Pheatra Wright	Mu	F	12		Daughter	S		At Home		
Biddy Wright	Mu	F	10		Daughter	S		At Home		
Easter Wright	Mu	F	6		Daughter	S				
Charles H Wright	Mu	M	2		Son	S				
Mellis Wright	Mu	F	2/12	May	Daughter	S				
June 18, 1880										
Dwelling #271/Family #281										
William H Dobbins	W	M	32			M		Farmer		
Rosa V Dobbins	W	F	29		wife	M		Keeping House		
James N Dobbins	W	M	3		Son	S				
Alvira Wright	W	F	26		Sister in law	S		At Home		
June 19, 1880										
Dwelling #286/Family #296										
Allain Wright	B	M	45			M		Farmer		
Nancy Wright	B	F	39		wife	M		Keeping House		
Lewis Wright	B	M	20		Son	S		At Home		Idiotic
Harriett Wright	B	F	16		Daughter	S		At Home		
Charlotte Wright	B	F	11		Daughter	S		At Home		
Allain Wright	B	M	6		Son	S				
Mary Willie Wright	B	F	3		Grand Daugh	S				

Appendix: Montgomery County, Virginia, 1880 Census

Name continued from previous page]	Attended School Within Year	Cannot Read	Cannot Write	Born	Father Born	Mother Born	Identification
56th Enumeration Dist **10th day of June, 1880**							
Dwelling #149/Family #184							
Nathaniel Wright		1	1	Virginia	Va	Va	
Elsey Wright		1	1	Virginia	Va	Va	
Pheatra Wright	1	1	1	Virginia	Va	Va	
Biddy Wright	1	1	1	Virginia	Va	Va	
Easter Wright				Virginia	Va	Va	
Charles H Wright				Virginia	Va	Va	
Mellis Wright				Virginia	Va	Va	
June 18, 1880							
Dwelling #271/Family #281							
William H Dobbins				Virginia	Va	Va	Alvira or Elvira A. Wright, daughter of James A. Wright (Floyd
Rosa V Dobbins				Virginia	Va	Va	County), granddaughter of Joseph Wright (Augusta County), and
James N Dobbins				Virginia	Va	Va	great granddaughter of 1826 Joseph Wright of Augusta County
Alvira Wright				Virginia	Va	Va	
June 19, 1880							
Dwelling #286/Family #296							
Allain Wright		1	1	Virginia	Va	Va	
Nancy Wright		1	1	Virginia	Va	Va	
Lewis Wright		1	1	Virginia	Va	Va	
Harriett Wright	1			Virginia	Va	Va	
Charlotte Wright		1	1	Virginia	Va	Va	
Allain Wright				Virginia	Va	Va	
Mary Willie Wright				Virginia	Va	Va	

Appendix: Montgomery County, Virginia, 1880 Census

Name	Color	Sex	Age	Month of Birth	Relationship	Marital Status	Married During Year	Occupation	Months Unem- ployed	Sickness Blind Deaf & Dumb Idiotic Disabled
Dwelling #273/Family #283										
John M Wright	W	M	42			M		Farmer		
Elmyria Wright	W	F	38		wife	M		Keeping House		
Lilly M Wright	W	F	8		Daughter	S				1
James W Wright	W	M	6		Son	S				
Peter F Wright	W	M	4		Son	S				

Appendix: Montgomery County, Virginia, 1880 Census

Name continued from previous page]	Attended School Within Year	Cannot Read	Cannot Write	Born	Father Born	Mother Born	Identification
Dwelling #273/Family #283							
John M Wright				Virginia	Va	Va	1902 John M. Wright of Montgomery County, son of James A.
Elmyria Wright				Virginia	Va	Va	Wright (Floyd County), grandson of Joseph Wright (Augusta
Lilly M Wright				Virginia	Va	Va	County), and great grandson of 1826 Joseph Wright of Augusta
James W Wright				Virginia	Va	Va	County
Peter F Wright				Virginia	Va	Va	

0769(010510)

1900 CENSUS

MONTGOMERY COUNTY, VIRGINIA

	Location				Relation				Personal Description						
In Cities	Number of dwelling houses in the order	Number of family in the order of	Name of each person whose place of abode on June 1, 1900, was	Relationship of each person the head of	Color			Date of Birth	Age at last	Whether single, married, widowed,	Number of years	Mother of how many	Number of these children
Street	House Number	of visitation	visitation	in this family.	the family	or race	Sex	Month	Year	birthday	or divorced	married	children	living

Alleghany District
June 14, 1900

		190	190	Harriett Wright	Head	W	F	Aug	1835	65	W	13	4	3
				Nicholas Wright	Son	W	M	Sep	1874	26	S			
				Edward Wright	Son	W	M	Mar	1876	24	S			
				Hattie Wright	Daughter	W	F	July	1878	22	S			

Alleghany Magisterial District
June 22, 1900

		348	350	Jack Wright	Head	B	M	May	1845	45	M	26	.	.
				Maggie Wright	Wife	B	F	June	1857	42	M	26	10	6
				Ruth Wright	Daughter	B	F	Mar	1889	11	S			
				Walter Wright	Son	B	M	Jan	1892	8	S			
				Ellen Wright	Daughter	B	F	Nov	1895	4	S			
				Lizzie Wright	Daughter	B	F	May	1897	3	S			

June 22, 1900

		261	262	Obadiah Wright	Head	W	M	Apr	1849	51	D	24	.	.
				Susan Waldon	Housekeeper	W	F	June	1842	59	W	1	3	3
				Mollie Waldon	Housekeeper	W	F	Apr	1869	31	S			
				Martha Waldon	Housekeeper	W	F	Nov	1873	27	S			
				Ora Waldon	Adopted	W	F	May	1892	7	S			

Auburn District
June 5, 1900

| | | 71 | 71 | Frank P Wright | Head | W | M | Mar | 1876 | 24 | M | 1 | . | . |
| | | | | Sallie B Wright | Wife | W | F | Apr | 1872 | 28 | M | 1 | 0 | 0 |

Appendix: Montgomery County, Virginia, 1900 Census

Name of each person whose place of abode on June 1, 1900, was in this family. [continued from prior page]	Nativity			Citizenship			Occupation, Trade, Or Profession of each person Ten Years of age and over.		Education		
	Place of birth of each person and parents of each person enumerated.			Year of immigration to the United States	Number of years in the United States	Naturalization			Attended school in months)	Can read	Can write	Can speak English
	Place of birth of this Person	Place of birth of Father of this person	Place of birth of Mother of this person				Occupation	Months not employed				
Harriett Wright	Virginia	Virginia	Virginia				Farmer			yes	yes	yes
Nicholas Wright	Virginia	Virginia	Virginia				Farm laborer			yes	yes	yes
Edward Wright	Virginia	Virginia	Virginia				R. R. laborer			yes	yes	yes
Hattie Wright	Virginia	Virginia	Virginia				.			yes	yes	yes
Jack Wright	Virginia	Virginia	Virginia				R.R. Laborer			no	no	yes
Maggie Wright	Virginia	Virginia	Virginia				.			no	no	yes
Ruth Wright	Virginia	Virginia	Virginia				at School			yes	yes	yes
Walter Wright	Virginia	Virginia	Virginia				at School			yes	no	yes
Ellen Wright	Virginia	Virginia	Virginia				.			no	no	yes
Lizzie Wright	Virginia	Virginia	Virginia				.			no	no	yes
Obadiah Wright	Virginia	Virginia	Virginia				Farmer	0		yes	yes	yes
Susan Waldon	Virginia	Virginia	Virginia				Housekeeper			no	no	yes
Mollie Waldon	Virginia	Virginia	Virginia				Housekeeper			yes	yes	yes
Martha Waldon	Virginia	Virginia	Virginia				Housekeeper			yes	yes	yes
Ora Waldon	Virginia	Virginia	Virginia				.			.	.	.
Frank T Wright	Virginia	Virginia	Virginia				Farm Laborer	0		yes	yes	yes
Sallie B Wright	Virginia	Virginia	Virginia							yes	yes	yes

| Name of each person whose place of abode on June 1, 1900, was in this family. [continued from prior page] | Ownership Of Home | | | | Identification |
	Owned or rented	Owned free or mortgaged	Farm or house	Number of farm schedule	
Harriett Wright Nicholas Wright Edward Wright Hattie Wright	O	F	F	102	
Jack Wright Maggie Wright Ruth Wright Walter Wright Ellen Wright Lizzie Wright	O	F	F	127	Jackson Wright, son of Calvin Wright and grandson of Harry Wright
Obadiah Wright Susan Waldon Mollie Waldon Martha Waldon Ora Waldon	O	F	F	153	
Frank P Wright Sallie B Wright	R		H		Peter Frank Wright, son of 1902 John M. Wright of Montgomery County, grandson of James A. Wright (Floyd County), great grandson of Joseph Wright (Augusta County), and great great grandson of 1826 Joseph Wright of Augusta County

Appendix: Montgomery County, Virginia, 1900 Census

In Cities Street	House Number	Number of dwelling houses in the order of visitation	Number of family in the order of visitation	Name of each person whose place of abode on June 1, 1900, was in this family.	Relationship of each person to the head of the family	Color or race	Sex	Month	Year	Age at last birthday	Whether single, married, widowed, or divorced	Number of years married	Mother of how many children	Number of these children living

Auburn District June 5, 1900

		72	72	John M Wright	Head	W	M	Feb	1838	61	M	0		
				Mary B Wright	Wife	W	F	July	1859	40	M	0	0	0
				Lillie M Wright	Daughter	W	F	Oct	1871	28	S			

Auburn District June 12, 1900

	317	331	332	John J Wright	Head	W	M	June	1870	29	M	4		
				Ada M Wright	Wife	W	F	Dec	1873	26	M	4	0	0
				Ann Krister(?)	M in law	W	F	Aug	1829	70	W		7	4

Auburn District June 12, 1900

		336	357	Robert Wright	Head	W	M	April	1833	67	W			
				Jenne Wright	Daughter	W	F	Dec	1872	27	Div		2	2
				Eugene Wright	Son	W	M	Jan	1874	26	S			
				Phillip R Wright	Son	W	M	Oct	1876	23	S			
				Hamey Wright	Son	W	M	Mar	1879	21	S			
				Harrie Wright	Son	W	M	Aug	1881	18	S			
				Jessie Wright	Grandson	W	M	Aug	1892	7	S			
				Johnie Wright	Grandson	W	M	Sept	1895	4	S			
				Sue Dean	Servant	W	F	May	1878	22	S			

Name of each person whose place of abode on June 1, 1900, was in this family. [continued from prior page]	Nativity			Citizenship			Occupation, Trade, Or Profession of each person Ten Years of age and over.		Education			
	Place of birth of each person and parents of each person enumerated.			Year of immigration to the United States	Number of years in the United States	Naturalization		Months not employed	Attended school in months)	Can read	Can write	Can speak English
	Place of birth of this Person	Place of birth of Father of this person	Place of birth of Mother of this person				Occupation					
John M Wright	Virginia	Virginia	Virginia				Farmer	0		yes	yes	yes
Mary B Wright	Virginia	Virginia	Virginia							yes	yes	yes
Lillie M Wright	Virginia	Virginia	Virginia							yes	yes	yes
John J Wright	Virginia	Virginia	Virginia				Engineer			yes	yes	yes
Ada M Wright	Virginia	Virginia	Virginia							yes	yes	yes
Ann Krister(?)	Virginia	Virginia	Virginia							yes	yes	yes
Robert Wright	Virginia	Virginia	Virginia				Machinist			yes	yes	yes
Jenne Wright	Virginia	Virginia	Virginia							yes	yes	yes
Eugene Wright	Virginia	Virginia	Virginia				Fireman R.R.			yes	yes	yes
Phillip R Wright	Virginia	Virginia	Virginia				Conductor			yes	yes	yes
Hamey Wright	Virginia	Virginia	Virginia				Brakeman			yes	yes	yes
Harrie Wright	Virginia	Virginia	Virginia				Engineer R.R.			yes	yes	yes
Jessie Wright	Virginia	Virginia	Virginia				.			.	.	.
Johnie Wright	Virginia	Virginia	Virginia				.			.	.	.
Sue Dean	Virginia	Virginia	Virginia				Cook			yes	yes	yes

Appendix: Montgomery County, Virginia, 1900 Census

Name of each person whose place of abode on June 1, 1900, was in this family. [continued from prior page]	Ownership Of Home				Identification
	Owned or rented	Owned free or mortgaged	Farm or house	Number of farm schedule	
John M Wright Mary B Wright Lillie M Wright	O	F	F	27	1902 John M. Wright of Montgomery County, son of James A. Wright (Floyd County, grandson of Joseph Wright (Augusta County), and great grandson of 1826 Joseph Wright of Augusta County
John J Wright Ada M Wright Ann Krister(?)	R		H		
Robert Wright Jenne Wright Eugene Wright Phillip R Wright Hamey Wright Harrie Wright Jessie Wright Sue Dean	R		H		

	Location				Relation				Personal Description						
In Cities		Number of dwelling houses in	Number of family in the	Name of each person whose place of abode	Relationship of each person						Age	Whether single, married,		Number Mother of	Number of these
Street	House Number	the order of visitation	order of visitation	on June 1, 1900, was in this family.	to the head of the family	Color or race	Sex	Date of Birth Month Year			at last birthday	widowed, or divorced	of years married	how many children	children living

Auburn District
June 15, 1900

		408	429	Alfred Stigad	Head	W	M	Mar	1843	57		M	15	.	.
				Evangline Stigad	Wife	W	F	Nov	1862	37		M	15	4	3
				Ada L. Stigad	Daughter	W	F	Mar	1887	13		S	.	.	.
				Roy E. Stigad	Son	W	M	Sept	1889	10		S	.	.	.
				Ruth M. Stigad	Son	W	M	Nov	1897	2		S	.	.	.
				Sarah F Wright	Aunt	W	F	May	1825	75		W	.	0	0

Auburn District
June 6, 1900

		119	127	Elijah Johnson	Head	W	M	Sept	1834	65		M	44	.	.
				Sarah Johnson	wife	W	F	May	1839	61		M	44	12	10
				Thomas H. Johnson	son	W	M	Mar	1879	21		S		.	.
				Walter Johnson	son	W	M	Mar	1884	16		S			
				Mary Wright	Daughter	W	F	Aug	1866	33		M	10	1	1
				Pearl Wright	Grandaughter	W	F	May	1891	9		S	.	.	.

Auburn District
June 6, 1900

8th		130	138	John S Wright	Head	W	M	Jan	1866	34		M	2	.	.
				Maggie Wright	Wife	W	F	Oct	1876	23		M	2	1	1
				Virginia Wright	Daughter	W	F	Dec	1898	1		S	.	.	.
				Sue Johnson	Servant	W	F	June	1876	24		M	.	.	.

Appendix: Montgomery County, Virginia, 1900 Census

Name of each person whose place of abode on June 1, 1900, was in this family. [continued from prior page]	Nativity Place of birth of each person and parents of each person enumerated.			Citizenship			Occupation, Trade, Or Profession of each person Ten Years of age and over.		Education		
	Place of birth of this Person	Place of birth of Father of this person	Place of birth of Mother of this person	Year of immigration to the United States	Number of years in the United States	Natural-ization	Occupation	Months not employed	Attended school in months)	Can read	Can write	Can speak English
Alfred Stigad	Virginia	Virginia	Virginia				Painter					
Evangline Stigad	Virginia	Virginia	Virginia							yes	yes	yes
Ada L. Stigad	Virginia	Virginia	Virginia							yes	yes	yes
Roy E. Stigad	Virginia	Virginia	Virginia							yes	yes	yes
Ruth M. Stigad	Virginia	Virginia	Virginia							yes	yes	yes
Sarah F Wright	Virginia	Virginia	Virginia							yes	yes	yes
Elijah Johnson	Virginia	Virginia	Virginia				Doctor	.		yes	yes	yes
Sarah Johnson	Virginia	Virginia	Virginia					.		yes	yes	yes
Thomas H. Johnson	Virginia	Virginia	Virginia				At school		9	yes	yes	yes
Walter Johnson	Virginia	Virginia	Virginia				At school		9	yes	yes	yes
Mary Wright	Virginia	Virginia	Virginia				.			yes	yes	yes
Pearl Wright	Virginia	Virginia	Virginia				.		.	.	.	.
John S Wright	England	England	England	1889	11	Pa	Broker per			yes	yes	yes
Maggie Wright	Virginia	Virginia	Virginia				.			yes	yes	yes
Virginia Wright	Illinois	England	Virginia				.		.	.	.	.
Sue Johnson	Virginia	Virginia	Virginia				Cook			yes	yes	yes

Name of each person whose place of abode on June 1, 1900, was in this family. [continued from prior page]	Ownership Of Home				Identification
	Owned or rented	Owned free or mortgaged	Farm or house	Number of farm schedule	
Alfred Stigad	R		H		
Evangline Stigad					
Ada L. Stigad					
Roy E. Stigad					
Ruth M. Stigad					
Sarah F Wright					
Elijah Johnson	O	F	H		
Sarah Johnson					
Thomas H. Johnson					
Walter Johnson					
Mary Wright					
Pearl Wright					
John S Wright	R		H		
Maggie Wright					
Virginia Wright					
Sue Johnson					

Appendix: Montgomery County, Virginia, 1900 Census

	Location				Relation			Personal Description						
In Cities	Number of dwelling houses in	Number of family in the	Name of each person whose place of abode	Relationship of each person					Age	Whether single, married,	Number	Mother of	Number of these
House	the order	order of	on June 1, 1900, was	the head of	Color		Date of Birth		at last	widowed,	of years	how many	children
Street Number	of visitation	visitation	in this family.	the family	or race	Sex	Month Year		birthday	or divorced	married	children	living

June 18, 1900

	497	518	Mary Wright	Head	C	F	May	1870	30	W	.	5	5
			Fletcher Wright	Son	C	M	Nov	1884	15	S			
			Johnnie M Wright	Son	C	M	Aug	1888	12	S			
			Charlie Wright	Son	C	M	Apr	1893	7	S			
			Margarett Wright	Daughter	C	F	Aug	1894	5	S			
			Clarance M Wright	Son	C	M	Aug	1896	3	S			

Auburn District
June 15, 1900

| | 429 | 450 | Johana Chandler | Head | W | F | Jan | 1865 | 35 | S | . | . | . |
| | | | Jennie Wright | Boarder | W | F | Apr | 1881 | 19 | M | 1 | 0 | 0 |

Name of each person whose place of abode on June 1, 1900, was in this family. [continued from prior page]	Nativity			Citizenship			Occupation, Trade, Or Profession of each person Ten Years of age and over.		Education			
	Place of birth of each person and parents of each person enumerated.			Year of immigra-tion to the United States	Number of years in the United States	Natural-ization						Can speak English
	Place of birth of this Person	Place of birth of Father of this person	Place of birth of Mother of this person				Occupation	Months not employed	Attended school in months)	Can read	Can write	
Mary Wright	Virginia	Virginia	Virginia				Washerwoman	.		yes	yes	yes
Fletcher Wright	Virginia	Virginia	Virginia				At school		9	yes	yes	yes
Johnnie M Wright	Virginia	Virginia	Virginia				Errand boy			yes	yes	yes
Charlie Wright	Virginia	Virginia	Virginia				.		.	.	.	.
Margarett Wright	Virginia	Virginia	Virginia				.		.	.	.	.
Clarance M Wright	Virginia	Virginia	Virginia				.		.	.	.	.
Johana Chandler	Virginia	Virginia	Virginia				Housekeeper			yes	yes	yes
Jennie Wright	Virginia	Virginia	Virginia				.			yes	yes	yes

Name of each person whose place of abode on June 1, 1900, was in this family. [continued from prior page]	Ownership Of Home				Identification
	Owned or rented	Owned free or mortgaged	Farm or house	Number of farm schedule	
Mary Wright					
Fletcher Wright					
Johnnie M Wright					
Charlie Wright					
Margarett Wright					
Clarance M Wright					
Johana Chandler	O	F	H		
Jennie Wright					

INDEX

Wright, John B, 34, 35
Wright, John H, 40, 41
Wright, John J, 59, 60, 61
Wright, John M, 36, 37, 51, 53, 59, 60, 61
Wright, John S, 62, 63, 64
Wright, John W, 48, 49
Wright, Johnie, 59, 60
Wright, Johnnie M, 65, 66, 67
Wright, Joseph, 6, 7, 8
Wright, Judith, 40, 41
Wright, Julia, 34, 48, 49
Wright, Lavinia, 30, 42, 43, 46, 47
Wright, Lennis, 34, 35
Wright, Levinia, 28
Wright, Lewis, 38, 39, 50, 51
Wright, Lillie M, 59, 60, 61
Wright, Lilly M, 52, 53
Wright, Lizzie, 56, 57, 58
Wright, Louisa, 38, 39, 40, 41
Wright, Lucy, 34, 35
Wright, Luther, 48, 49
Wright, Maggie, 56, 57, 58, 62, 63, 64
Wright, Maggie J, 46, 47
Wright, Margarett, 65, 66, 67
Wright, Margret, 48, 49
Wright, Mark S, 34, 35
Wright, Martha, 40, 41
Wright, Martin J, 40, 41, 46, 47
Wright, Mary, 36, 37, 40, 41, 48, 49, 62, 63, 64, 65, 66, 67
Wright, Mary A, 36, 37, 40, 41
Wright, Mary B, 59, 60, 61
Wright, Mary M, 34, 35
Wright, Mary Willie, 50, 51
Wright, Mathew, 36, 37
Wright, Medora J, 34, 35
Wright, Mellis, 50, 51
Wright, Nancy, 31
Wright, Nancy, 38, 39, 50, 51
Wright, Nancy C, 46, 47

Wright, Nanney C, 40, 41
Wright, Naoma L, 34, 35
Wright, Nathaniel, 36, 37, 50, 51
Wright, Nicholas, 56, 57, 58
Wright, Nicholis H, 46, 47
Wright, Obadiah, 56, 57, 58
Wright, Pearl, 62, 63, 64
Wright, Peggy, 36, 37, 38, 39
Wright, Peter F, 52, 53
Wright, Pheatra, 50, 51
Wright, Phillip R, 59, 60, 61
Wright, Phoebe, 36, 37
Wright, Reed, 6, 7, 8
Wright, Reubin, 40, 41
Wright, Richard, 9, 10, 11
Wright, Robert, 59, 60, 61
Wright, Ruth, 56, 57, 58
Wright, Sallie B, 56, 57, 58
Wright, Samuel, 6, 7, 8, 46, 47
Wright, Samuel L, 40, 41
Wright, Sarah, 28
Wright, Sarah F, 62, 63, 64
Wright, Sir Francis G., 6, 7, 8
Wright, Smith, 14, 15, 16, 17, 18
Wright, Theodore F, 30
Wright, Thomas, 38, 39
Wright, Thomas L, 40, 41
Wright, Virginia, 28, 30, 62, 63, 64
Wright, Virginia A, 34, 35
Wright, Walter, 56, 57, 58
Wright, Wheeler T, 40, 41
Wright, William, 28, 30, 42, 43
Wright, William C, 34, 35
Wright, William F, 30

WRIGHT FAMILY

LAND GRANTS

1776 TO 1900

MONTGOMERY COUNTY, VIRGINIA

Revised as of June 30, 2011

This document is an appendix to a larger work titled <u>Sorting Some Of The Wrights Of Southern Virginia</u>. The work is divided into parts for each family of Wrights that has been researched. Each part is divided into two sections; the first section is text discussing the family and the evidence supporting the relationships and the second section is a descendants chart summarizing the relationships and information known about each individual.

The appendices to the work (of which this document is one) present source records for persons named Wright by county and by type of record with the identification of the person named and their Wright ancestors to the extent known.

The sources for the records listed in this appendix are the following:

1) Virginia, Index to Patents 1623-1774, Alphabetically and by Book, microfilm #29308, Genealogical Society of the Church of Jesus Christ of the Latter Day Saints and Patent Deeds available from The Virginia State Library, Richmond, Virginia 23219.

The identification of a person or their ancestor by year and county indicates their year of death and county of residence at death. For example, "1763 Thomas Wright of Bedford County" indicates that this was the Thomas Wright who died in 1763 in Bedford County. If no state is listed after the county, the state is Virginia; counties in states other than Virginia will have a state listed after the county, as in "1876 William S. Wright of Highland County, Ohio".

A parenthetical after the name indicates an identification of the person when a place of death is not yet known, as in "John Wright (Goochland County Carpenter)". A county in parentheses after the name indicates the county with which that person was most identified when no evidence of the place of death has yet been found, as in "Grief Wright (Bedford County)".

All or portions of the text and descendants charts for each Wright family identified are available from the author:

Robert N. Grant
15 Campo Bello Court   (H) 650-854-0895
Menlo Park, California 94025   (O) 650-614-3800

This is a work in process and I would be most interested in receiving additional information about any of the persons identified in these records in order to correct any errors or expand on the information given.

Appendix: Montgomery County, Virginia, Land Grants

Book/Page	Date	Name	Description	Identification
O/450	1785/04/21	Richard Wright	400 acres on Turkey Fork of Elk Creek, a branch of New River	1819 Richard Wright of Grayson County
087/454	1837/10/16	Amos Wright	68 acres on Wilson's Creek off North Fork of Roanoke River	Amos Wright, son of Sarah Wright and grandson of 1826 Joseph Wright of Augusta County
114/738	1858/05/01	Amos Wright	8 acres	Amos Wright, son of Sarah Wright and grandson of 1826 Joseph Wright of Augusta County
120/365	1888/09/08	John M. Wright Wm. H. Dobbins	5-7/8 acres on Bush Creek	1902 John M. Wright of Montgomery County, son of James A. Wright (Floyd County), grandson of Joseph Wright (Augusta County), and great grandson of 1826 Joseph Wright of Augusta County

WRIGHT FAMILY

DEED RECORDS

1776 TO 1900

MONTGOMERY COUNTY, VIRGINIA

Revised as of June 30, 2011

This document is an appendix to a larger work titled <u>Sorting Some Of The Wrights Of Southern Virginia</u>. The work is divided into parts for each family of Wrights that has been researched. Each part is divided into two sections; the first section is text discussing the family and the evidence supporting the relationships and the second section is a descendants chart summarizing the relationships and information known about each individual.

The appendices to the work (of which this document is one) present source records for persons named Wright by county and by type of record with the identification of the person named and their Wright ancestors to the extent known.

The sources for the records listed in this appendix are the following:

1) Montgomery County, Virginia, Index to Deeds and Deeds, microfilms #___, Genealogical Society of the Church of Jesus Christ of the Latter Day Saints.

2) <u>Annals of Southwest Virginia, 1769-1800</u>, by Lewis Preston Summers, Genealogical Publishing Co., Inc., Baltimore, Maryland, 1970.

3) <u>Montgomery County, Va Deed Book A 1773-1789</u>, by James L. Douthat, Mountain Press, P.O. Box 400, Signal Mountain, Tennessee 37377-0400, 1987.

The identification of a person or their ancestor by year and county indicates their year of death and county of residence at death. For example, "1763 Thomas Wright of Bedford County" indicates that this was the Thomas Wright who died in 1763 in Bedford County. If no state is listed after the county, the state is Virginia; counties in states other than Virginia will have a state listed after the county, as in "1876 William S. Wright of Highland County, Ohio".

A parenthetical after the name indicates an identification of the person when a place of death is not yet known, as in "John Wright (Goochland County Carpenter)". A county in parentheses after the name indicates the county with which that person was most identified when no evidence of the place of death has yet been found, as in "Grief Wright (Bedford County)".

All or portions of the text and descendants charts for each Wright family identified are available from the author:

Robert N. Grant
15 Campo Bello Court   (H) 650-854-0895
Menlo Park, California 94025   (O) 650-614-3800

This is a work in progress and I would be most interested in receiving additional information about any of the persons identified in these records in order to correct any errors or expand on the information given.

Appendix: Montgomery County, Virginia, Deed Records:

Book/Page		Date	Grantor	Grantee	Instrument	Identification
C	340	1800/09/10	John Wright & Mary Wright	Nathaniel Crandell	Deed	John Wright (Montgomery County), son of 1815 Joseph Wright of Bedford County and grandson of 1763 Thomas Wright of Bedford County
F	409	1818/02/14	Barbee Miller	George Wright	Deed	
IJ	046	1824/11/11	John Wood & Mary Wood	Hiram Wright	Deed	
IJ	320	1826/02/11	Hiram Wright & Elizabeth Wright	Jacob Helms	Deed	
K	543	1831/01/06	Abijah Booth & Rodah Booth	William T. Wright	Deed	
L	196	1833/12/13	Samuel Lucas & Catharine Lucas	Amos Wright	Deed	Amos Wright, son of Sarah Wright and grandson of 1826 Joseph Wright of Augusta County
L	278	1834/06/10	Amos Wright & Levinia Wright	Cornelious Hall	Deed	Amos Wright, son of Sarah Wright and grandson of 1826 Joseph Wright of Augusta County
M	065	1836/02/21	James Hedge & George Hodge	William Wright	Deed	
M	478	1838/12/29	Amos Wright & Levenia Wright	Dudley G Reed	Deed	Amos Wright, son of Sarah Wright and grandson of 1826 Joseph Wright of Augusta County
M	472	1839/03/18	Amos Wright & Levenia Wright	John Haymaker	Deed	Amos Wright, son of Sarah Wright and grandson of 1826 Joseph Wright of Augusta County
M	654	1840/10/17	Horatio Smith	Amos Wright	Deed	Amos Wright, son of Sarah Wright and grandson of 1826 Joseph Wright of Augusta County
M	631	1840/09/02	Charles Yearout & Elizabeth Yearout	Amos Wright	Deed	Amos Wright, son of Sarah Wright and grandson of 1826 Joseph Wright of Augusta County

Appendix: Montgomery County, Virginia, Deed Records:

Book/Page		Date	Grantor	Grantee	Instrument	Identification
M	672	1840/12/26	Amos Wright & Levenia Wright	Daniel Aker	Deed	Amos Wright, son of Sarah Wright and grandson of 1826 Joseph Wright of Augusta County
O	278	1846/09/22	Joseph Wright & Mary Wright	John Wright	Deed	Grantor: 1856 Joseph Wright of Roanoke County, son of John Wright (Montgomery County), grandson of 1815 Joseph Wright of Bedford County, and great grandson of 1763 Thomas Wright of Bedford County Grantee: John B. Wright, son of 1856 Joseph Wright of Roanoke County, grandson of John Wright (Montgomery County), great grandson of 1815 Joseph Wright of Bedford County, and great great grandson of 1763 Thomas Wright of Bedford County
O	253	1846/01/06	Daniel Wright & Eliza D. P. Wright & Joel W. Peppers & Mary J. Peppers & William C. Taylor & Mary L. Taylor & Arthur J. McCorkle & Roger H. Abbott & Sarah H. Abbott	Williamson Burton	Deed	Daniel Wright, son of Harry Wright
P	001	1850/04/01	Daniel Wright & Eliza D. P. Wright & Joel W. Peppers & Mary J. Peppers & William C. Taylor & Mary L. Taylor & Arthur J. McCorkle & Roger H. Abbott & Sarah H. Abbott	George P. Pepper	Deed	Daniel Wright, son of Harry Wright
P	249	1841/05/01	William N. Bullard	Amos Wright	Deed	Amos Wright, son of Sarah Wright and grandson of 1826 Joseph Wright of Augusta County
P	237	1843/02/14	Jotham Pearce	Amos Wright	Deed	Amos Wright, son of Sarah Wright and grandson of 1826 Joseph Wright of Augusta County

Appendix: Montgomery County, Virginia, Deed Records:

Book/Page		Date	Grantor	Grantee	Instrument	Identification
P	249	1841/05/01	Amos Wright & Lavenia Wright	William N. Bullard	Deed	Amos Wright, son of Sarah Wright and grandson of 1826 Joseph Wright of Augusta County
P	426	1854/05/26	William St. Clair	Theodore F. Wright, Trustee	D.T.	Theodrick or Theodore F. Wright, son of 1845 William Wright of Franklin County, grandson of 1830 William Wright of Franklin County, great grandson of 1809 William Wright of Franklin County, great great grandson of 1792 John Wright of Fauquier County, and possibly great great great grandson of John Wright (Westmoreland County Overseer)
Q	024	1856/02/25	Theodore F Wright, Trustee	Samuel McConkey & James M. G. Kent	Deed	Theodrick or Theodore F. Wright, son of 1845 William Wright of Franklin County, grandson of 1830 William Wright of Franklin County, great grandson of 1809 William Wright of Franklin County, great great grandson of 1792 John Wright of Fauquier County, and possibly great great great grandson of John Wright (Westmoreland County Overseer)
Q	029	1856/03/06	Michael S. Poff	Theodore F. Wright, Trustee	D.T.	Theodrick or Theodore F. Wright, son of 1845 William Wright of Franklin County, grandson of 1830 William Wright of Franklin County, great grandson of 1809 William Wright of Franklin County, great great grandson of 1792 John Wright of Fauquier County, and possibly great great great grandson of John Wright (Westmoreland County Overseer)
Q	299	1858/02/16	John H. Wright & Camilla S. Wright & Eli Phlegar, Trustee & William C. Hagan, Trustee	Samuel D. Stuart	Deed	John H. Wright, son of 1841 Price Wright of Bedford County, grandson of 1835 Benjamin Wright of Bedford County, great grandson of 1814 John Wright of Bedford County, and great great grandson of John Wright (Goochland County Carpenter)

Appendix: Montgomery County, Virginia, Deed Records:

Book/Page		Date	Grantor	Grantee	Instrument	Identification
Q	456	1858/12/16	Daniel Wright & Elizabeth D. P. Wright & Joel W. Peppers & Mary Jane Peppers & Arthur J. McCorkle & Naomi McCorkle & Mary Melvina Vermillion & William P. Taylor & James J. Taylor & Jesse W. Taylor & J. T. S. Baird & Louisa Baird & Louisa Abbott & Lizzie Abbott	T. H. Barnes	Deed	Daniel Wright, son of Harry Wright
Q	389	1859/02/07	Amos Wright & Levenia Wright	Adam Earheart	Deed	Amos Wright, son of Sarah Wright and grandson of 1826 Joseph Wright of Augusta County
Q	452	1858/12/16	Daniel Wright & Elizabeth D. P. Wright & Joel W. Peppers & Mary Jane Pappers & Arthur McCorkle & Naomi McCorkle & Mary Melvina Vermillion & William P. Taylor & James J. Taylor & Jesse W. Taylor & J. T. S. Baird & S. Louisa Baird & Louisa Abbott & Lizzie Abbott	Cyrus Farrow	Deed	Daniel Wright, son of Harry Wright

Appendix: Montgomery County, Virginia, Deed Records:

Book/Page		Date	Grantor	Grantee	Instrument	Identification
Q	454	1858/12/16	Daniel Wright & Elizabeth D. P. Wright & Joel W. Peppers & Mary Jane Pappers & Arthur McCorkle & Naomi McCorkle & Mary Melvina Vermillion & William P. Taylor & James J. Taylor & Jesse W. Taylor & J. T. S. Baird & S. Louisa Baird & Louisa Abbott & Lizzie Abbott	Michael Butt	Deed	Daniel Wright, son of Harry Wright
Q	518	1860/04/07	Durman vs Durman, William C. Hagan, Comr.	Amos Wright	Deed	Amos Wright, son of Sarah Wright and grandson of 1826 Joseph Wright of Augusta County
R	046A	1861/02/06	Amos Wright & Levenia Wright	Crockett L. Pierce	Deed	Amos Wright, son of Sarah Wright and grandson of 1826 Joseph Wright of Augusta County
R	046B	1861/02/21	Amos Wright & Lavenia Wright	Augustus A Hobson	Deed	Amos Wright, son of Sarah Wright and grandson of 1826 Joseph Wright of Augusta County
R	101	1861/11/06	William C. Hagan, Trustee	Amos Wright	Deed	Amos Wright, son of Sarah Wright and grandson of 1826 Joseph Wright of Augusta County
R	116	1862/02/03	Amos Wright & Levenia Wright	William M. Barnitz, Trustee	D.T.	Amos Wright, son of Sarah Wright and grandson of 1826 Joseph Wright of Augusta County
R	157	1862/09/14	Allsup Wright &	Jacob B. Moses	Deed	Alsup Wright, son of Grief Wright (Bedford County)
R	250	1863/10/19	Amos Wright & Levenia Wright	Joseph D. Feather	Deed	Amos Wright, son of Sarah Wright and grandson of 1826 Joseph Wright of Augusta County

Appendix: Montgomery County, Virginia, Deed Records:

Book/Page		Date	Grantor	Grantee	Instrument	Identification
S	455	1870/07/04	John M Gibson	John M. Wright	Agreement	Probably 1902 John M. Wright of Montgomery County, son of James A. Wright (Floyd County), grandson of Joseph Wright (Augusta County), and great grandson of 1826 Joseph Wright of Augusta Count
S	615	1872/11/00	Mercine B. Wright & John W. Furrow, attorney in fact for Mercina B. Wright & Charles E. Collins & John T. Collins & Samuel K. Collins	George Palmer	Deed	
S	641	1871/03/18	Amos Wright & Lavinia Wright & David G. Douthat & Mary A. Douthat	Minnis Headen	Deed	Amos Wright, son of Sarah Wright and grandson of 1826 Joseph Wright of Augusta County
T	161	1873/04/02	John M. Gibson & Olive M. Gibson	John M. Wright	Deed	Probably 1902 John M. Wright of Montgomery County, son of James A. Wright (Floyd County), grandson of Joseph Wright (Augusta County), and great grandson of 1826 Joseph Wright of Augusta County
U	022	1874/08/01	Polly Wright & Robert C. Slocum & Cynthia Cunningham & Elliott P. Cunningham & Sally Harrison & John R. Gray & Malinda D. Gray	Esther A. Crockett	P.A.	
V	403	1879/11/12	William A Goins	John M. Wright	B of S	Probably 1902 John M. Wright of Montgomery County, son of James A. Wright (Floyd County), grandson of Joseph Wright (Augusta County), and great grandson of 1826 Joseph Wright of Augusta County

Appendix: Montgomery County, Virginia, Deed Records:

Book/Page		Date	Grantor	Grantee	Instrument	Identification
V	483	1874/12/05	Thomas E. Sullivan, Commissioner in D. Wright et al v. Gordon Dobbins et al	Gordon Dobbins	Deed	
W	369	1881/05/07	William G Guerrant & Bettie R. Guerrant	John M. Wright	Deed	Probably 1902 John M. Wright of Montgomery County, son of James A. Wright (Floyd County), grandson of Joseph Wright (Augusta County), and great grandson of 1826 Joseph Wright of Augusta County
Y	494	1885/07/21	O. B. Wright	Lee, Taylor & Snead	Crop Lien	
26	108	1886/11/19	Wm G Guerrant & Bettie R. Guerrant	John M. Wright	Deed	Probably 1902 John M. Wright of Montgomery County, son of James A. Wright (Floyd County), grandson of Joseph Wright (Augusta County), and great grandson of 1826 Joseph Wright of Augusta County
28	320	1888/12/24	Anderson Watkins & Lucy J. Watkins	Bettie Wright & Gathlic Walker & Bessie Walker	Deed	
28	504	1878/06/14	Sublett vs Anderson	Also Wright	Deed	Alsup Wright, son of Grief Wright (Bedford County)
37	080	1890/09/23	William D Kirkwood & Emma J. Kirkwood	Jack Wright	Deed	
41	012	1892/07/13	Bettie Wright	Green Carden or Carter	Deed	
41	010	1888/12/24	Anderson Watkins & Lucy J. Watkins	Bettie Wright	Deed	
39	354	1891/12/11	R. A. Wright & Amanda M. Wright	F. M. Jones, Tr	D.T.	Robert A. Wright, son of 177 Joseph Wright of Bedford County
43	409	1895/10/15	O. B. Wright	Susan Waldron	Deed	

Appendix: Montgomery County, Virginia, Deed Records:

Book/Page		Date	Grantor	Grantee	Instrument	Identification
43	420	1895/11/02	John M. Wright & Elmira Wright	Wm. H. Dobbins	Deed	1902 John M. Wright of Montgomery County, son of James A. Wright (Floyd County), grandson of Joseph Wright (Augusta County), and great grandson of 1826 Joseph Wright of Augusta County
44	205	1893/04/11	H. D. Wade & Bettie M. Wade	J. Wright	Deed	
45	186	1897/11/05	J. W. Helm & Emma C. Helm	Calvin Wright	Deed	
44	500	1897/03/24	O. B. Wright	C. T. Furrow	Mortgage	

Appendix: Montgomery County, Virginia, Deed Records:

Book/Page	Date	Grantor	Grantee	Instrument	Identification
47 046	1899/12/01	Caroline S. Wright & A. G. Franklin & S. M. Franklin & Thomas M. Franklin & B. H. Franklin & Bettie L. Witt & Mary McAlister & Jn. B. Franklin & Sue Shuffleberger & J. A. Franklin & J. S. Franklin & Jn. H. Franklin & Mary A. Vanslaw & Martha J. Sublett & Mollie J. W. Franklin C. H. Dudley & E. A. Dudley & John L. Dudley & Janie D. Dudley & Mollie E. Franklin & Lucy L. Tyler & J. R. Bean & Cora V. Fairburn & James F. Bean & W. J. Bean & Sadie Bean & Sam'l Bean & Alice Bean & Emma W. Zink & J. A. Birchfield & Rosa B. Whiteseaver & Elizabeth H. Suffleberger & E. H. Stanley & John H. Birchfield & Alvasi Jones & Ida Coffee	Bettie L. Witt et al	Decree of Partition	Caroline S. (Franklin) Wright

INDEX

WRIGHT FAMILY

LAND TAX LISTS

1782 TO 1850

MONTGOMERY COUNTY, VIRGINIA

Revised as of June 24, 2011

This document is an appendix to a larger work titled <u>Sorting Some Of The Wrights Of Southern Virginia</u>. The work is divided into parts for each family of Wrights that has been researched. Each part is divided into two sections; the first section is text discussing the family and the evidence supporting the relationships and the second section is a descendants chart summarizing the relationships and information known about each individual.

The appendices to the work (of which this document is one) present source records for persons named Wright by county and by type of record with the identification of the person named and their Wright ancestors to the extent known.

The source for the records listed in this appendix is the following:

   1)   Montgomery County, Virginia, Land Tax Lists, available from The Library of Virginia, 11th & Capitol Streets, Richmond, Virginia 23219-3491.

The identification of a person or their ancestor by year and county indicates their year of death and county of residence at death. For example, "1763 Thomas Wright of Bedford County" indicates that this was the Thomas Wright who died in 1763 in Bedford County. If no state is listed after the county, the state is Virginia; counties in states other than Virginia will have a state listed after the county, as in "1876 William S. Wright of Highland County, Ohio".

A parenthetical after the name indicates an identification of the person when a place of death is not yet known, as in "John Wright (Goochland County Carpenter)". A county in parentheses after the name indicates the county with which that person was most identified when no evidence of the place of death has yet been found, as in "Grief Wright (Bedford County)".

All or portions of the text and descendants charts for each Wright family identified are available from the author:

       Robert N. Grant
       15 Campo Bello Court   (H) 650-854-0895
       Menlo Park, California 94025 (O) 650-614-3800

This is a work in progress and I would be most interested in receiving additional information about any of the persons identified in these records in order to correct any errors or expand on the information given.

1782 LAND TAX LIST

MONTGOMERY COUNTY, VIRGINIA

Appendix: Montgomery County, Virginia, 1782 Land Tax List:

[No title headings in original]

[Name]		[Acres]		[Tax?]	Identification
Richard Wright	1'6	400	30	6	1819 Richard Wright of Grayson County

1787 LAND TAX LIST

MONTGOMERY COUNTY, VIRGINIA

Appendix: Montgomery County, Virginia, 1787 Land Tax List:

[No headings in original]

[Name]	[Acres]		[Tax]	Identification
List A				
Richd Wright	400	30	9.0	1819 Richard Wright of Grayson County
List B				
No Wrights listed				
List C				
No Wright listed				

LAND TAX LISTS FOR 1788 THROUGH 1820

MONTGOMERY COUNTY, VIRGINIA

Appendix: Montgomery County, Virginia, 1788 thru 1820 Land Tax Lists:

[No title headings in original]

[Name]	[Acres]	[Tax?]	Identification
No Wrights listed			

1821 LAND TAX LIST

MONTGOMERY COUNTY, VIRGINIA

Appendix: Montgomery County, Virginia, 1821 Land Tax List:

William Currin District:

Name of owners	Residence	Estate whether held in fee simple or for life &c.	Number of Acres	Description of the Land	Distance & bearing from the Court house	Value of land pr Acre including buildings	Sum added to the land on acct of buildings	Total Value of the Land and buildings
John Wright	Montgomery	By deed	100	adj P. Heaverer	6 SW	3.50	100	350.00

Appendix: Montgomery County, Virginia, 1821 Land Tax List:

William Currin District:

Names of owners [Continued from prior page]	Amt. of Tax at the rate of	Explanation of alterations during the Preceeding Year	Identification
John Wright	.32		John Wright (Montgomery County), son of 1815 Joseph Wright of Bedford County and grandson of 1763 Thomas Wright of Bedford County

Appendix: Montgomery County, Virginia, 1821 Land Tax List:

John B Goodrich District:

Name of Owner	Residence	Estate	No of Acres	Description of the land	Distance and bear-ing from the ct. hs.	Value of land p acre including buildings $ cts	Sum added to the land on act of buildings $ cts	Total Value of the land & buildings	Amount of tax at the rate of $ cts	Explanation of alterations during the preceding _____ _____	Identification

[No Wrights listed]

1822 LAND TAX LIST

MONTGOMERY COUNTY, VIRGINIA

Appendix: Montgomery County, Virginia, 1822 Land Tax List:

William Currin District:

Names of Owners	Residence	Estate whether held in fee simple for Life &c.	Number of Acres	Description of the Land	Distance& bearing from the Court House	Value of land per Acre including Buildings	Sum added to the Land on Acct of Buildings	Total Value of the Land & buildings
John Wright	Montgomery	By deed	100	Adj. sd. Heavere	16 SW	3.50	100	350.00

Appendix: Montgomery County, Virginia, 1822 Land Tax List:

William Currin District:

Names of Owners [Continued from prior page]	Amt. of Tax at the Rate of 9 Cents per Acre	Explanation of alterations during the preceding Year	Identification
John Wright	.32		John Wright (Montgomery County), son of 1815 Joseph Wright of Bedford County and grandson of 1763 Thomas Wright of Bedford County

Appendix: Montgomery County, Virginia, 1822 Land Tax List:

J. B. Goodrich District:

						Value of land p acre includ- ing buildings $____ cts	Sum added to the land on account of the buildings $____ cts	Total Value $ cts	Total amt. of Taxes $ cts		Identification

[No Wrights listed]

1823 LAND TAX LIST

MONTGOMERY COUNTY, VIRGINIA

Appendix: Montgomery County, Virginia, 1823 Land Tax List:

William Currin District:

Names of Owners	Residence	Estate whether held in fee simple for Life &c.	Numbers of Acres	Description of the Land	Distance& Bearing from the Court House	Value of Land per Acre including Buildings	Sum added to the Land on Account of Buildings	Total Value of the Land and Buildings
John Wright	Montgomery	By deed	100	Adj. P. Heavners	16 SW	3.50	100	350.00

Appendix: Montgomery County, Virginia, 1823 Land Tax List:

William Currin District:

Names of Owners [Continued from prior page]	Amount of Tax at the Rate of 5 per- cent per $100 Value		Identification
John Wright	.28		John Wright (Montgomery County), son of 1815 Joseph Wright of Bedford County and grandson of 1763 Thomas Wright of Bedford County

Appendix: Montgomery County, Virginia, 1823 Land Tax List:

John B. Goodrich District:

Name of Owner	Residence	Estate &c	No of Acres of Land	Description of the Land	Distance & bearing from the court house	Value of land per acre $ cts	Sum added to the Land on account of the buildings $ cts	Total Value $ cts	Amount of tax on the whole tract $ cts		Identification

[No Wrights listed]

1824 LAND TAX LIST

MONTGOMERY COUNTY, VIRGINIA

Appendix: Montgomery County, Virginia, 1824 Land Tax List:

James Barnett District:

Names of Owners	Residence	in fee	No. of _____ of Land	Description of the Land	Distance & Bearing from C.H.	Value of Land pr Acre Including Buildings	Sum added to the land on account of Buildings	Total of Land & Buildings		
John Wright	Montgy		110	Adjn. P. Heavener	16 SW	3.50	100	385.00		
George Wright	Unknown		112	On Jacob Harmon	26 S	1.00		102.	0	0

Appendix: Montgomery County, Virginia, 1824 Land Tax List:

James Barnett District:

Names of Owners [Continued from prior page]	Amt of Tax		Identification
John Wright	.31	Rectified from 100 Acres	John Wright (Montgomery County), son of 1815 Joseph Wright of Bedford County and grandson of 1763 Thomas Wright of Bedford County
George Wright	.09	Omitted part off T. Harmon	

Appendix: Montgomery County, Virginia, 1824 Land Tax List:

John B. Goodrich District:

_____	Residence	Estate	Number of Acres	Description of the land	distance and bearing from the ct. House	Value of land p acre including buildings $ cts	Sum added to the land on account of buildings $ cts	Total value of the land & buildings	Amount of tax at the rate of ___ $ cts	Explanation of alterations during the preceding year	Identification

[No Wrights listed]

1825 LAND TAX LIST

MONTGOMERY COUNTY, VIRGINIA

Appendix: Montgomery County, Virginia, 1825 Land Tax List:

James Barnett District:

Names of Owners	Residence	No. of Acres	Description of the land	Distance & bearing from the C.H.	V. pr ac.	Added on account of Buildings	Total Valuation of land		
John Wright	Mont.	110	Adjg. P. Heavener	16 SW	3.50	100	385.00		
George Wright	Unknown	112	Jacob Harmon	26 S	1.00		112.	0	0

Appendix: Montgomery County, Virginia, 1825 Land Tax List:

James Barnett District:

Names of Owners [Continued from prior page]	Tax of Land		Identification
John Wright	.31		John Wright (Montgomery County), son of 1815 Joseph Wright of Bedford County and grandson of 1763 Thomas Wright of Bedford County
George Wright	.09		

Appendix: Montgomery County, Virginia, 1825 Land Tax List:

John B Goodrich District:

Name of Owner	Residence	Estate &c	Num-ber of Acres	Description of the Land	Distance & bear-ing from the court house	Value of land per acre includ-ing buildings $ cts	Sum added to the land on act of Buildings $ cts	Total value of the land & buildings $ cts	Amount of tax on land &c $ cts		Identification

[No Wrights listed]

1826 LAND TAX LIST

MONTGOMERY COUNTY, VIRGINIA

Appendix: Montgomery County, Virginia, 1826 Land Tax List:

Samuel Shields District:

[No Headings in Original]

John Wright	Montg.	110	Adj. P. Heavener	16 SW	3.50	100	385.00		
George Wright	Montg	112	Jacob Harmons	26 S	1.00		112.	0	0

Appendix: Montgomery County, Virginia, 1826 Land Tax List:

Samuel Shields District:

[Continued from prior page]		Identification
John Wright	.31	John Wright (Montgomery County), son of 1815 Joseph Wright of Bedford County and grandson of 1763 Thomas Wright of Bedford County
George Wright	.09	

Appendix: Montgomery County, Virginia, 1826 Land Tax List:

John B Goodrich District:

						$ cts	$ cts	$ cts	$ cts		Identification

[No Wrights listed]

1827 LAND TAX LIST

MONTGOMERY COUNTY, VIRGINIA

Appendix: Montgomery County, Virginia, 1827 Land Tax List:

Samuel Shields District:

Name of Owners	Residence	How held	No. of Acres	Description of the land	Distance and bearing from the court house	Value per Acre	Added on account of Building	Total Valuation of land		
John Wright	Montg		110	adj. P. Heavners	16 SW	3.50	100	385.00		
George Wright	Mont		112	Jacob Harmons	26 S	1.00	75	112.	0	0

Appendix: Montgomery County, Virginia, 1827 Land Tax List:

Samuel Shields District:

Name of Owners [Continued from prior page]	Amount of Tax	Remarks &c	Identification
John Wright	.31		John Wright (Montgomery County), son of 1815 Joseph Wright of Bedford County and grandson of 1763 Thomas Wright of Bedford County
George Wright	.09		

Appendix: Montgomery County, Virginia, 1827 Land Tax List:

Robert S Currin District:

Names of Owners	Residence	Estate	Number of acres of land	Description of the Land	Distance & Bearing from the Court House	Value of land per acre $ cts	Improve- ments $ cts	Total amount of land with the improvements $ cts	Amount of Tax $ cts		Identification

[No Wrights listed]

1828 LAND TAX LIST

MONTGOMERY COUNTY, VIRGINIA

Appendix: Montgomery County, Virginia, 1828 Land Tax List:

Samuel Shields District:

Name of Owners	Residence	How held	No. of Acres	Description of the Land	Distance and bearing from the court house	Value per Acre $ cts	Add on Account of Building	Total Valuation of Land		
John Wright	Montg		110	adj P. Heavners	16 SW	3.50	100	385.00		
George Wright	Unkn		112	Waters Jacob Harmons	26 S	1.00	75	112.	0	0

Appendix: Montgomery County, Virginia, 1828 Land Tax List:

Samuel Shields District:

Name of Owners [Continued from prior page]	Total Amount of Tax	Remarks &c &c &c	Identification
John Wright	.31		John Wright (Montgomery County), son of 1815 Joseph Wright of Bedford County and grandson of 1763 Thomas Wright of Bedford County
George Wright	.09		

Appendix: Montgomery County, Virginia, 1828 Land Tax List:

R. S Currin District:

Names of Owners	Residence	Estate	Number of acres of Land	Discription of Land	Distance & bearing from the CH	Value of land per Acre $ cts	Improve- ments $ cts	Total Amount of land with the Improvements $ cts	Amount of Taxes $ cts		Identification

[No Wrights listed]

1829 LAND TAX LIST

MONTGOMERY COUNTY, VIRGINIA

Appendix: Montgomery County, Virginia, 1829 Land Tax List:

William Wade District:

Name of Owner of land	Residence	Estate How held	Number of Acres	Description of Land	Distance and bearing from the court house	Value of land per acre	Amount added on account of Buildings	Total Valuation of Land		
John Wright	Montg		110	adj P. Heavners	16 SW	3.50	75	385.00		
George Wright	Unkn		112	adj Jacob Harmons	26 S	1.00	75	112.	0	0

Appendix: Montgomery County, Virginia, 1829 Land Tax List:

William Wade District:

Name of Owner of land [Continued from prior page]	Amount of Tax on Land	Remarks &c &c	Identification
John Wright	.31		John Wright (Montgomery County), son of 1815 Joseph Wright of Bedford County and grandson of 1763 Thomas Wright of Bedford County
George Wright	.09		

Appendix: Montgomery County, Virginia, 1829 Land Tax List:

____ District:

Name of Owner	Residence	Estate	Num-ber of Acres	Description of the Land	Distance & Bearing from the Court House	Value of land per Acre $ cts	Amount Added on the land on account of buildings $ cts	Total Value $ cts	Amount of Taxes $ cts	____	Identification

[No Wrights listed]

1830 LAND TAX LIST

MONTGOMERY COUNTY, VIRGINIA

Appendix: Montgomery County, Virginia, 1830 Land Tax List:

Samuel Shields District:

Name of Owners of Land	Residence	Estate held	Number of Acres	Description of the Land	distance and bearing from the court house	Rate of the land per acre $ Cts	Added on Account of Buildings	Total Value of Land $ Cts		
John Wright	Montg		110	adj P. Heavners	16 SW	3.50	75	385.00		
George Wright	Unkn		112	adj Jacob Harmons	26 S	1.00	75	112.	0	0

Appendix: Montgomery County, Virginia, 1830 Land Tax List:

Samuel Shields District:

Names of Owners of Land [Continued from prior page]	Amount of Tax on Land	Remarks &c &c	Identification
John Wright	.31		John Wright (Montgomery County), son of 1815 Joseph Wright of Bedford County and grandson of 1763 Thomas Wright of Bedford County
George Wright	.09		

Appendix: Montgomery County, Virginia, 1830 Land Tax List:

William Wade District:

Name of Owner	Residence	Estate	Number of Acres	Description of land	Distance & bearing from the Court house	Value of the land per acre $ cts	Amount added on account Building $ cts	Total Value of Land $ cts	Amount of Tax on Land $ cts	Remarks &c &c	Identification

[No Wrights listed]

1831 LAND TAX LIST

MONTGOMERY COUNTY, VIRGINIA

Appendix: Montgomery County, Virginia, 1831 Land Tax List:

____ Howard District:

Name of Owners of Land	Residence	Estate how held	Number of Acres	Description of the Land	distance and bearing from the court house	Rate of land per acre $ cts	Added on account of buildings $ Cts	Total value of the land $ Cts
John Wright	Montg		110	adj P. Heavner	16 SW	3.50	75	385.00

Appendix: Montgomery County, Virginia, 1831 Land Tax List:

_____ Howard District:

Names of Owners of Land [Continued from prior page]	Amount of Tax on Land	Remarks &c	Identification
John Wright	.31		John Wright (Montgomery County), son of 1815 Joseph Wright of Bedford County and grandson of 1763 Thomas Wright of Bedford County

Appendix: Montgomery County, Virginia, 1831 Land Tax List:

William Wade District:

Name of Owners	Residence		Number of Acres	description of Land	Distance & bearing from C.H.	Value of Land per acre	Amount added on account of buildings	Total Value of Land	Amount of Tax on Land	Remarks &c &c	Identification

[No Wrights listed]

1832 LAND TAX LIST

MONTGOMERY COUNTY, VIRGINIA

Appendix: Montgomery County, Virginia, 1832 Land Tax List:

William H. Horne District:

Name of Owners	Residence	Estate how held	Number of Acres	Description of the land	Distance and bearing from the the Court House	Value of land per Acre	Amount added on account of building	Total Value of the land
John Wright	Montg		110	adj P. Heavner	16 SW	3.50	75	385.00

Appendix: Montgomery County, Virginia, 1832 Land Tax List:

William H. Horne District:

Name of Owners [Continued from prior page]	Amount of Tax on the land	Remarks &c	Identification
John Wright	.31		John Wright (Montgomery County), son of 1815 Joseph Wright of Bedford County and grandson of 1763 Thomas Wright of Bedford County

Appendix: Montgomery County, Virginia, 1832 Land Tax List:

William Wade District:

Name of Owners	Residence	Number of Acres	Local description of land	Distance & bearing from C House	Value of Land per acre $ cts	amt added on account of Buildings $ cts	Total Value of Land $ cts	Total Amount of Tax $ cts	Remarks &c &c	Identification

[No Wrights listed]

1833 LAND TAX LIST

MONTGOMERY COUNTY, VIRGINIA

Appendix: Montgomery County, Virginia, 1833 Land Tax List:

Samuel Shields District:

Name of persons	Residence	Estate how held	Number of acres		Distance & bearing from the court house	Value of land pr acre	Amount added on account of the buildings	Total value of land
John Wright	Montg		110	Adj P. Heavner	16 SW	3.50	75	385.00

Appendix: Montgomery County, Virginia, 1833 Land Tax List:

Samuel Shields District:

Name of persons [Continued from prior page]	Amount of tax on the land	Remarks &c &c	Identification
John Wright	.31		John Wright (Montgomery County), son of 1815 Joseph Wright of Bedford County and grandson of 1763 Thomas Wright of Bedford County

Appendix: Montgomery County, Virginia, 1833 Land Tax List:

_____ District:

Name of Owner	Residence	___	Number of Acres	Local description of Land	distance & bearing from C House	Value of Land per acre $ cts	Amt. added on account of buildings $ cts	Total Value of Land $ cts	Total Amt. of Tax $ cts	Remarks &c &c	Identification

[No Wrights listed]

1834 LAND TAX LIST

MONTGOMERY COUNTY, VIRGINIA

Appendix: Montgomery County, Virginia, 1834 Land Tax List:

William Wade District:

Name of Owner	Residence	Number of Acres	Local description &c	distance & bearing from the C.H.	Value of Land pr acre $ Cts	Amt. added on account of building $ Cts	Total value of Land $ Cts
Amos Wright	Montg	250	Wilsons Creek	4 N	4.00	250	1000.00
" "	"	41	" "	"	5.00	"	205.00
" "	"	64	" "	"	5.00	"	320.00
" "	"	76	" "	"	2.50	"	190.00
" "	"	27	" "	"	.25	"	6.75
" "	"	22	" "	"	.50	"	11.00

Appendix: Montgomery County, Virginia, 1834 Land Tax List:

William Wade District:

Name of Owner [Continued from prior page]	Total amt of Tax $ Cts	Remarks &c	Identification
Amos Wright	.80	deed from S. Lucas	Amos Wright, son of Sarah Wright and grandson of 1826 Joseph Wright of Augusta County
" "	.17	do do	
" "	.26	do do	
" "	.16	do do	
" "	.01	do do	
" "	.01	do do	

Appendix: Montgomery County, Virginia, 1834 Land Tax List:

Samuel Shields District:

Names of Persons	Residence	Estate how held	Number of Acres		Distance and bearing from the Court House	Waters of Land per Acre	Amount added on account of Buildings	Total Value of the Land
John Wright	Montg		100	adj P Heaveners	16 SW	3.50	75	385.00

Appendix: Montgomery County, Virginia, 1834 Land Tax List:

Samuel Shields District:

Names of Persons [Continued from prior page]	Amount of Tax on the land	Remarks &c	Identification
John Wright	.31		John Wright (Montgomery County), son of 1815 Joseph Wright of Bedford County and grandson of 1763 Thomas Wright of Bedford County

1740(062411)

1835 LAND TAX LIST

MONTGOMERY COUNTY, VIRGINIA

Appendix: Montgomery County, Virginia, 1835 Land Tax List:

William Wade District:

Name of Owners	Residence	No. of Acres	description & local Situation	distance & bearing from C.H.	Value of Land per acre $ Cts	Amt. added on account of Building $ Cts	Total Value of Land $ Cts
Amos Wright	Montg	59	Wilsons Creek	4 N	5.00	200	295.00
" "	"	41	" "	"	5.00	"	205.00
" "	"	64	" "	"	5.00	"	320.00
" "	"	76	" "	"	2.50	"	190.00
" "	"	27	" "	"	.25	"	6.75
" "	"	22	" "	"	.50	"	11.00

Appendix: Montgomery County, Virginia, 1835 Land Tax List:

William Wade District:

Name of Owners [Continued from prior page]	Total amt of Tax $ Cts	Remarks &c &c	Identification
Amos Wright	.24		Amos Wright, son of Sarah Wright and grandson of 1826 Joseph Wright of Augusta County
" "	.17		
" "	.26		
" "	.16		
" "	.01		
" "	.01		

Appendix: Montgomery County, Virginia, 1835 Land Tax List:

Samuel Shields District:

Names of Owners	Residence	Estate How Held	Number of Acres		Distance & bearing from the C. House	Waters of land per Acre	Amount added on account of buildings	Total Value of The Land
John Wright	Montg		110	adj P. Heaveners	16 SW	3.50	75	385.00

Appendix: Montgomery County, Virginia, 1835 Land Tax List:

Samuel Shields District:

Names of Owners [Continued from prior page]	Amount of Tax On the Land	Remarks &c	Identification
John Wright	.31		John Wright (Montgomery County), son of 1815 Joseph Wright of Bedford County and grandson of 1763 Thomas Wright of Bedford County

1740(0624111)

1836 LAND TAX LIST

MONTGOMERY COUNTY, VIRGINIA

Appendix: Montgomery County, Virginia, 1836 Land Tax List:

Charles B. Gardner District:

Name of Owner	Residence	No. of Acres	Description & local situation	distance & bearing from C.H.	Value of land per acre $: Cts	Amt. added on acct. of buildings $: Cts	Total Amt. of land includ- ing buildings $: Cts
Amos Wright	Montg	59	Wilson Creek	4 N	5.00	200	295.00
" "	"	41	" "	"	5.00	"	205.00
" "	"	64	" "	"	5.00	"	320.00
" "	"	76	" "	"	2.50	"	190.00
" "	"	27	" "	"	.25	"	6.75
" "	"	22	" "	"	.50	"	11.00

Appendix: Montgomery County, Virginia, 1836 Land Tax List:

Charles B. Gardner District:

Name of Owner [Continued from prior page]	Total Amt. of Tax $: Cts	Remarks &c &c	Identification
Amos Wright	.24		Amos Wright, son of Sarah Wright and grandson of 1826 Joseph Wright of Augusta County
" "	.17		
" "	.26		
" "	.16		
" "	.01		
" "	.01		

Appendix: Montgomery County, Virginia, 1836 Land Tax List:

Samuel Shields District:

Names of Owners	Residence	Estate How Held	Number of Acres		Distance and bearing from the C House	Waters of Land per Acre	Amount added on account of buildings	Total Value of The Land
John Wright	Montg		110	adj P. Heaveners	16 SW	3.50	75	385.00

Appendix: Montgomery County, Virginia, 1836 Land Tax List:

Samuel Shields District:

Names of Owners [Continued from prior page]	Amount of Tax On the Land	Remarks &c	Identification
John Wright	.31		John Wright (Montgomery County), son of 1815 Joseph Wright of Bedford County and grandson of 1763 Thomas Wright of Bedford County

1740(062411)

1837 LAND TAX LIST

MONTGOMERY COUNTY, VIRGINIA

Appendix: Montgomery County, Virginia, 1837 Land Tax List:

Samuel Shields District:

Name of Owner	Residence	Estate	Number of acres of Land	Descriptions of the Land & its Local situation	Distance & bearing from the C. House	Rate of the Same per acre $ cts	Amount added on account of buildings $ cts	Total Value of the Land $ cts	Amount of Tax on the Land $ cts	Remarks &c	Identification
John Wright	Montg		110	Adj P. Heavens	16 SW	3.50	100	385.00	.31		John Wright (Montgomery County), son of 1815 Joseph Wright of Bedford County and grandson of 1763 Thomas Wright of Bedford County

Appendix: Montgomery County, Virginia, 1837 Land Tax List:

Charles B. Gardner District:

Name of Owner	Residence	No. Lot	Name of Town	Amount added on account of buildings $ ¢	Value of lot including the buildings $ ¢	Yearly rent of the House & Lot $ Cts	Total Amt. of of Tax $ Cts	Remarks &c	Identification
Daniel Wright	Montg	24		50.00	25.00	15.00	.02	Will of William Peppers	
" "	"	24		50.00	30.00	15.00	.03	Same	

1740(062411)

1838 LAND TAX LIST

MONTGOMERY COUNTY, VIRGINIA

Appendix: Montgomery County, Virginia, 1838 Land Tax List:

Charles B. Gardner District:

Name of Owner	Residence	No. of Acres	Description & Local Situation	Distance & Bearing from C.H.	Value of Land per Acre $: Cts	Amt. added on acct. of buildings $: Cts	Total Value of Land including buildings $: Cts
Amos Wright	Montg	59	Wilson Creek	4 N	5.00	200.00	295.00
	"	41		"	5.00	"	205.00
	"	64		"	5.00	"	320.00
	"	76		"	2.50	"	190.00
	"	27		"	.25	"	6.75
	"	22		"	.50	"	11.00
	"	68		"	.50	"	34.00

Appendix: Montgomery County, Virginia, 1838 Land Tax List:

Charles B. Gardner District:

Name of Owner [Continued from prior page]	Total Amount of Tax $	Cts	Remarks	Identification
Amos Wright	.30			Amos Wright, son of Sarah Wright and grandson of 1826 Joseph Wright of Augusta County
	.21			
	.32			
	.19			
	.01			
	.02			
	.04		New Grant	

Appendix: Montgomery County, Virginia, 1838 Land Tax List:

Samuel Shields District:

Names of Owners	Residence	Estate	Number of acres of Land	Description of the Land & its local Situation	Description and bearing from the C. House	Rate of the land per acre	Amount added On account or Buildings	Total Value of the land
John Wright	Montg		110	Adj P. Heaveners	16 SW	3.50	100	385.00

Appendix: Montgomery County, Virginia, 1838 Land Tax List:

Samuel Shields District:

Name of Owner [Continued from prior page]	Amount of Tax On the land	Remarks &c	Identification
John Wright	.39		John Wright (Montgomery County), son of 1815 Joseph Wright of Bedford County and grandson of 1763 Thomas Wright of Bedford County

Appendix: Montgomery County, Virginia, 1838 Land Tax List:

Charles B. Gardner District:

Name of Owner	Residence	No. Lot	Name of Town	Amount added on account of buildings $ ¢	Value of lot including the buildings $ ¢	Yearly rent of the House & Lot $ Cts	Total Amt. of of Tax $ Cts	Remarks &c	Identification
Daniel Wright	Montg	24		50.00	25.00	15.00	.03		
" "	"	24		50.00	34.00	15.00	.03		

1839 LAND TAX LIST

MONTGOMERY COUNTY, VIRGINIA

Appendix: Montgomery County, Virginia, 1839 Land Tax List:

Charles B. Gardiner District:

Name of Owners	Residence	No. of Acres	Description & Local Situation	Distance & bearing from C.H.	Value of Land per Acre $: Cts	Amt. added on acct. of Buildings $: Cts	Total value of Land including buildings $: Cts
Amos Wright	Montg	59	Wilson Creek	4 N	5.00	200.00	295.00
	"	41		"	5.00	"	205.00
	"	64		"	5.00	"	320.00
	"	76		"	2.50	"	190.00
	"	27		"	.25	"	6.75
	"	22		"	.50	"	11.00
	"	68		"	.50	"	34.00

Appendix: Montgomery County, Virginia, 1839 Land Tax List:

Charles B. Gardiner District

Name of Owners [Continued from prior page]	Total Amt. Tax $ Cts	Remarks &c	Identification
Amos Wright	.30 .21 .32 .19 .01 .02 .04		Amos Wright, son of Sarah Wright and grandson of 1826 Joseph Wright of Augusta County

Appendix: Montgomery County, Virginia, 1839 Land Tax List:

Charles B. Gardner District:

Name of Owner	Residence	No. Lot	Name of Town	Amount added on account of buildings $ ¢	Value of lot including the buildings $ ¢	Yearly rent of the House & Lot $ Cts	Total Amt. of of Tax $ Cts	Remarks &c	Identification
Daniel Wright	Berkley	23.24	Lafayette	50.00	30.00	15.00	.03		
" "	"	10	"	50.00	30.00	15.00	.03		

Appendix: Montgomery County, Virginia, 1839 Land Tax List:

Samuel Sh__ District:

Names of Owners	Residence	Estate	Number of Acres of Land	Description of the land __ local Situations	Distance & bearing from C.H.	Rate of the Land $ cts	amount added on account of buildings $ cts	Total Value of the Land $ cts	Amount of Tax on the Land $ cts	Remarks &c &c	Identification
[No Wrights listed]											

Appendix: Montgomery County, Virginia, 1839 Land Tax List:

Western District:

Name of Owners	Residence	Estate how held	Number of Acres of Land	Descrip- tion and Local Situation of Land	Distance and bearing from the Court House	Value of land per acre under last apraisement including buildings	Sum added to land on account of building under last Apartment	Present value of land per acre including buildings	Sum added to the present value of land on account of buildings		Identification
John Wright			110	Highwa_	16 S	3.50		3.00			John Wright (Montgomery County), son of 1815 Joseph Wright of Bedford County and grandson of 1763 Thomas Wright of Bedford County

1840 LAND TAX LIST

MONTGOMERY COUNTY, VIRGINIA

Appendix: Montgomery County, Virginia, 1840 Land Tax List:

Waddy G. Curren District:

Names of Owners	Residence	head of Estate	No. of Acres	Description & Situation of Land	Distance and Bearing from the Court house	Value of land per acre including Buildings	Sum added on account of Buildings	Total Value of land and Buildings

[No Wrights listed]

Appendix: Montgomery County, Virginia, 1840 Land Tax List:

Waddy G. Curren District:

Names of Owners [Continued from prior page]	Total Amount of Tax	Remarks	Identification

[No Wrights listed]

Appendix: Montgomery County, Virginia, 1840 Land Tax List:

Waddy G. Currin District:

Name of Owner	Residence	In fee		Name of Town	Value of ld including Buildings	Sum added to the Value of lot on account of Buildings	Yearly rent of houses & Lot
Daniel Wright	Berkley	23 & 24				100.00	
"		10				40.00	

Appendix: Montgomery County, Virginia, 1840 Land Tax List:

Waddy G. Currin District:

Name of Owners [Continued from prior page]	Total Amount of Tax	Remarks	Identification
Daniel Wright	.10		
"	.04		

Appendix: Montgomery County, Virginia, 1840 Land Tax List:

Charles B Gardner District:

Name of Owners	Residence	Kind of Estate	No of Acres	Description or Situation of Land	Distance & bearing C.H.	Value of land per acre including Buildings $ Cts	Sum added on account of Buildings $ Cts	Total Value of Land & Buildings $ Cts	Total Amount of Tax $ Cts	Remarks	Identification
Amos Wright	Montg	In fee	135	Wilson Creek	4 N	5.25	400	700.75	.71	190 & 32 acres transfered to Haymaker & Reed (leaving the ballance of 7 smal tracts)	Amos Wright, son of Sarah Wright and grandson of 1826 Joseph Wright of Augusta County

1841 LAND TAX LIST

MONTGOMERY COUNTY, VIRGINIA

Appendix: Montgomery County, Virginia, 1841 Land Tax List:

Waddy G. Curren District:

Name of Owners	Residence	Estate how held	No. of Acres	Description of the Land, as to Water Courses Mountains & Contiguous tracts	Distance & bearing from Court House	Value of land per acre includ- ing Buildings	Sum added on Account of Buildings	Total Value of Land and Buildings
Amos Wright			49	Waters Elliotts Creek	2 SW	3.00		147.00
			144¾		3	5.00		723.75

Appendix: Montgomery County, Virginia, 1841 Land Tax List:

Waddy G. Curren District:

Name of Owners [Continued from prior page]	Total Amount of Tax	Explanation of alterations during the preceding year especially whom transferred	Identification
Amos Wright	.19	Deed from Horitia Smith 1841	Amos Wright, son of Sarah Wright and grandson of 1826 Joseph Wright of Augusta County
	.91	Deed from Charles Gearant 1841	

Appendix: Montgomery County, Virginia, 1841 Land Tax List:

Waddy G. Curren District:

Name of Owner	Residence	Estate how held	No. of Lot in plan of Town	Name of Town	Value of Buildings	Value of lot including Buildings	Yearly Rent of Lot
Daniel Wright	Berkley		½ of 23 & 24			100.00	
"			10			40.00	

Appendix: Montgomery County, Virginia, 1841 Land Tax List:

Waddy G. Curren District:

Name of Owners [Continued from prior page]	Total Amount of Tax on Lot	Explanation of alterations during the preceding Year	Identification
Daniel Wright	.13		
"	.05		

Appendix: Montgomery County, Virginia, 1841 Land Tax List:

Charles B. Gardner District:

Name of Owner	Residence	Estate how held	No of Acres	Description of the Land, as to water courses, Mountains, and contiguous tracts &c	Distance & bearing from C.H.	Value of land per acre including Buildings $ Cts	Sum added on account of Buildings $ Cts	Total value of Land & Buildings $ Cts

[No Wrights listed]

Appendix: Montgomery County, Virginia, 1841 Land Tax List:

Charles B. Gardner District:

Name of Owner [continued from prior page]	Total Amount of Tax $ Cts	Explanation of Alterations during the preceeding year especially from whom transferred	Identification

[No Wrights listed]

1740(062411)

1842 LAND TAX LIST

MONTGOMERY COUNTY, VIRGINIA

Appendix: Montgomery County, Virginia, 1842 Land Tax List:

Waddy G. Curren District:

Name of Owner	Residence	Estate how held	No. of Acres	Description of Land as to water courses Mountains & contiguous tracts	Distance and bearing from C. house	Value of land per acre including buildings $ Cts	Sum added on account of Buildings $ Cts	Total Value of Land and buildings $ Cts
Amos Wright			49	Waters Elliotts Creek	3 S	3.00		147.00
			144¼		3 S	5.00		723.75

Appendix: Montgomery County, Virginia, 1842 Land Tax List:

Waddy G. Curren District:

Name of Owner [Continued from prior page]	Total Amount of Tax $ Cts	Explanation of alterations during the preceding year especially from whom transferred	Identification
Amos Wright	.19	Deed from Horatio Smith 1841	Amos Wright, son of Sarah Wright and grandson of 1826 Joseph Wright of Augusta County
	.91	Deed from Charles Gearant 1841	

Appendix: Montgomery County, Virginia, 1842 Land Tax List:

Waddy G. Curren District:

Name of Owner	Residence	Estate how held	No. of Lot	Name of Town	Value of Buildings $ Cts	Value of lot including Buildings $ Cts	Yearly Rent of Lot $ Cts
Daniel Wright	Berkley		½ of 23 & 24			100.00	
"			10			40.00	

Appendix: Montgomery County, Virginia, 1842 Land Tax List:

Waddy G. Curren District:

Name of Owners [Continued from prior page]	Amount of Tax $ Cts	Remarks Explanation of alterations during the preceeding year	Identification
Daniel Wright	.13		
"	.05		

Appendix: Montgomery County, Virginia, 1842 Land Tax List:

Charles B. Gardner District:

Name of Owner	Residence	Estate how held	No of Acres	Description of Land as to water courses, Mountains, & contiguous tracts &c	Distance and bearing from C. House	Value of Land per acre including Buildings $ Cts	Sum added on account of Buildings $ Cts	Total value of Land & Buildings $ Cts
[No Wrights listed]								

Appendix: Montgomery County, Virginia, 1842 Land Tax List:

Charles B. Gardner District:

Name of Owner [continued from prior page]	Total Amount of Tax $ Cts	Explanation of alterations during the preceeding year, especially from whom transferred	Identification

[No Wrights listed]

1843 LAND TAX LIST

MONTGOMERY COUNTY, VIRGINIA

Appendix: Montgomery County, Virginia, 1843 Land Tax List:

Waddy G. Curren District:

Name of Owner	Residence	Estate how held	No. of Acres	Description of Land as to water courses Mountains and contiguous tracts	Distance and bearing from C.H.	Value of Land per Acre including Buildings $ Cts	Sum added on Account of Buildings $ Cts	Total Value of Land and Buildings $ Cts
Amos Wright			49		3 S	3.00		147.00
			144¼		3 S	5.00		723.75

Appendix: Montgomery County, Virginia, 1843 Land Tax List:

Waddy G. Curren District:

Name of Owners [Continued from prior page]	Total amount of Tax $ Cts	Explanation of Alterations during the preceding year especially from whom transferred	Identification
Amos Wright	.23	Deed from Horatio Smith 1841	Amos Wright, son of Sarah Wright and grandson of 1826 Joseph Wright of Augusta County
	1.09	Deed from Charles Gearant 1841	

Appendix: Montgomery County, Virginia, 1843 Land Tax List:

Waddy G. Curren District:

Name of Owner	Residence	Estate how held	No. of Lot	Name of Town	Value of Buildings $ Cts	Value of lot includ- ing- Buildings $ Cts	Yearly Rent of Lot &c $ Cts
Daniel Wright	Berkley		½ of 23 & 24			100.00	
"			10			40.00	

Appendix: Montgomery County, Virginia, 1843 Land Tax List:

Waddy G. Curren District:

Name of Owners [Continued from prior page]	Amount of Tax $ Cts	Remarks Explanation of Alterations during the preceeding year especially to whom transferred	Identification
Daniel Wright	.15		
"	.06		

Appendix: Montgomery County, Virginia, 1843 Land Tax List:

Charles B. Gardner District:

Name of Owner	Residence	Estate how held	No of Acres	Description of land, as to water courses, Mountains, & contiguous tracts &c	Distance and bearing from C. House	Value of Land per acre including Buildings $ Cts	Sum added on account of Buildings $ Cts	Total value of Land & Buildings $ Cts

[No Wrights listed]

Appendix: Montgomery County, Virginia, 1843 Land Tax List:

Charles B. Gardner District:

Name of Owner [continued from prior page]	Total Amount of Tax $ Cts	Explanation of Alterations during the preceeding year, especially from whom transferred	Identification

[No Wrights listed]

1844 LAND TAX LIST

MONTGOMERY COUNTY, VIRGINIA

Appendix: Montgomery County, Virginia, 1844 Land Tax List:

Waddy G. Curren District:

Name of Owners	Residence	Estate how held	No. of Acres	Description of Land as to Water Courses Mountains and contiguous Tracts	Distance and bearing from C.House	Value of Land per Acre including Buildings $ Cts	Sum added on Account of Building $ Cts	Total Value of Land and Buildings $ Cts
Amos Wright			49	Waters Elliotts Creek	3 S	3.00		147.00
			144¼		3 S	5.00		723.75

Appendix: Montgomery County, Virginia, 1844 Land Tax List:

Waddy G. Curren District:

Name of Owners [Continued from prior page]	Total Amount of Tax $ Cts	Explanation of Alterations during the preceding year from whom transferred	Identification
Amos Wright	.19	Deed from Horatio Smith 1841	Amos Wright, son of Sarah Wright and grandson of 1826 Joseph Wright of Augusta
	.90	Deed from Charles Gearant 1841	County

Appendix: Montgomery County, Virginia, 1844 Land Tax List:

Waddy G. Curren District:

Names of Owners	Residence	Estate how held	No. of Lot	Names of Towns	Value of Buildings	Value of Lots including Buildings	Yearly rent of Lot &c
Daniel Wright	Berkley		½ of 23 & 24			100.00	
"			10			40.00	

Appendix: Montgomery County, Virginia, 1844 Land Tax List:

Waddy G. Curren District:

Names of Owners [Continued from prior page]	Amount of Tax	Remarks Explanation of Alterations during the preceeding year especially to whom transfered	Identification
Daniel Wright	.13		
"	.06		

Appendix: Montgomery County, Virginia, 1844 Land Tax List:

Charles B. Gardner District:

Name of Owner	Residence	Estate how held	No of Acres	Description of Land as to water courses, Mountains, & contiguous tracts &c	Distance and bearing from C. House	Value of Land per acre including Buildings $ Cts	Sum added on account of Buildings $ Cts	Total value of Land & Buildings $ Cts

[No Wrights listed]

Appendix: Montgomery County, Virginia, 1844 Land Tax List:

Charles B. Gardner District:

Name of Owner [continued from prior page]	Total amt. of Tax $ Cts	Explanation of alterations during the preceeding year, especially from whom transferred	Identification

[No Wrights listed]

1740(062411)

1845 LAND TAX LIST

MONTGOMERY COUNTY, VIRGINIA

Appendix: Montgomery County, Virginia, 1845 Land Tax List:

Waddy G. Curren District:

Name of Owner	Residence	Estate, whether held in fee simple, for life, &c	No. of Acres	Description of the land as to watercourses, mountains and contiguous tracts	Distance and bearing from the courthouse	Value of land per acre including buildings	Sum added to the land on account of buildings	Total value of the land and buildings
Amos Wright			49		3 S	3.00		147.00
			144¾		3 S	5.00		723.75

Appendix: Montgomery County, Virginia, 1845 Land Tax List:

Waddy G. Curren District:

Name of Owner [Continued from prior page]	Am't of tax on the whole tract, at the legal rate	Explanation of alterations during the preceding year, especially from whom transferred	Identification
Amos Wright	.15	Deed from Horatio Smith 1841	Amos Wright, son of Sarah Wright and grandson of 1826 Joseph Wright of Augusta
	.73	Deed from Charles Gearant 1841	County

Appendix: Montgomery County, Virginia, 1845 Land Tax List:

Waddy G. Currin District:

Name of Owner	Residence	Estate whether held in fee simple, for life, &c	Number of each lot in the Town	Name of Town	Value of buildings	Value of lots including buildings	Yearly rent of lots
Daniel Wright	Berkley		½ of 23 & 24			100.00	
"			10			40.00	

Appendix: Montgomery County, Virginia, 1845 Land Tax List:

Waddy G. Currin District:

Name of Owner [Continued from prior page]	Am't of tax on lots, at the legal rate	Explanation of alterations during the preceding year	Identification
Daniel Wright	.14		
"	.04		

Appendix: Montgomery County, Virginia, 1845 Land Tax List:

Charles B. Gardner District:

Name of Owner	Residence	Estate whether held in fee simple for life &c	No. of Acres	Description of land, as to water courses, mountains, and contiguous tracts	Distance and bearing from the court house	Value of Land per acre, including buildings	Sum added to the land account of buildings	Total value of the land and buildings

[No Wrights listed]

Appendix: Montgomery County, Virginia, 1842 Land Tax List:

Charles B. Gardner District:

Name of Owner [continued from prior page]	Am't of tax on the whole tract at the legal rate	Explanation of alterations during the preceeding year, especially from whom transferred	Identification

[No Wrights listed]

1846 LAND TAX LIST

MONTGOMERY COUNTY, VIRGINIA

Appendix: Montgomery County, Virginia, 1846 Land Tax List:

Waddy G. Curren District:

Name of Owner	Residence	Estate, whether held in fee simple, for life, &c	No. of Acres	Description of the land as to watercourses, mountains and contiguous tracts	Distance and bearing from the courthouse	Value of land per acre including buildings	Sum added to the land on account of buildings	Total value of the land and buildings
Amos Wright		49		3 S	3.00	147.00		
		145		3 S	5.00	724.00		

Appendix: Montgomery County, Virginia, 1846 Land Tax List:

Waddy G. Curren District:

Name of Owner [Continued from prior page]	Am't of tax on the whole tract, at the legal rate	Explanation of alterations during the preceding year, especially from whom transferred	Identification
Amos Wright	.15	Deed from H Smith 1841	Amos Wright, son of Sarah Wright and grandson of 1826 Joseph Wright of
	.73	Deed from Chas Gearant 1841	Augusta County

Appendix: Montgomery County, Virginia, 1846 Land Tax List:

Waddy G. Curren District:

Name of Owner	Residence	Estate whether held in fee sim-ple, for life, &c	Number of each lot in the Town	Name of Town	Value of buildings	Value of lots includ-ing buildings	Yearly rent of lots
Daniel Wright	Berkley		½ of 23 & 24			100.00	
"			10			40.00	

Appendix: Montgomery County, Virginia, 1846 Land Tax List:

Waddy G. Curren District:

Name of Owner [Continued from prior page]	Am't of tax on lots, at the legal rate	Explanation of alterations during the preceding year	Identification
Daniel Wright	.10		
"	.04		

Appendix: Montgomery County, Virginia, 1846 Land Tax List:

Charles B. Gardner District:

Name of Owner	Residence	Estate whether held in fee simple for life &c	No. of Acres	Description of land, as to water courses, mountains, and contiguous tracts	Distance and bearing from the court house	Value of Land per acre, including buildings	Sum added to the land account of buildings	Total value of the land and buildings
[No Wrights listed]								

Appendix: Montgomery County, Virginia, 1846 Land Tax List:

Charles B. Gardner District:

Name of Owner [continued from prior page]	Am't of tax on the whole tract at the legal rate	Explanation of alterations during the preceeding year, especially from whom transferred	Identification

[No Wrights listed]

1740(062411)

1847 LAND TAX LIST

MONTGOMERY COUNTY, VIRGINIA

Appendix: Montgomery County, Virginia, 1847 Land Tax List:

Waddy G. Curin District:

Name of Owner	Residence	Estate, whether held in fee simple, for life, &c	No. of Acres	Description of the land as to watercourses, mountains and contiguous tracts	Distance and bearing from the courthouse	Value of land per acre including buildings	Sum added to the land on account of buildings	Total value of the land and buildings
Amos Wright			49	Waters Elliotts Creek	3 S	3.00		147.00
			145		3 S	5.00		724.00

Appendix: Montgomery County, Virginia, 1847 Land Tax List:

Waddy G. Curin District:

Name of Owner [Continued from prior page]	Am't of tax on the whole tract, at the legal rat	Explanation of alterations during the preceding year, especially from whom transferred	Identification
Amos Wright	.61 .73	Deed from H Smith 1841 Deed from Chs Gearant 1841	Amos Wright, son of Sarah Wright and grandson of 1826 Joseph Wright of Augusta County

Appendix: Montgomery County, Virginia, 1847 Land Tax List:

Waddy G. Curin District:

Name of Owner	Residence	Estate whether held in fee simple, for life, &c	Number of each lot in the Town	Name of Town	Value of buildings	Value of lots including buildings	Yearly rent of lots
Daniel Wright	Berkley		½ of 23 & 24			100.00	
"			10			40.00	

Appendix: Montgomery County, Virginia, 1847 Land Tax List:

Waddy G. Curin District:

Name of Owner [Continued from prior page]	Am't of tax on lots, at the legal rate	Explanation of alterations during the preceding year	Identification
Daniel Wright	.10		
"	.04		

Appendix: Montgomery County, Virginia, 1847 Land Tax List:

C. B. Gardner District:

Name of Owner	Residence	Estate whether held in fee simple for life &c	No. of Acres	Description of land, as to water courses, mountains, and contiguous tracts	Distance and bearing from the court house	Value of Land per acre, including buildings	Sum added to the land account of buildings	Total value of the land and buildings
[No Wrights listed]								

Appendix: Montgomery County, Virginia, 1847 Land Tax List:

C. B. Gardner District:

Name of Owner [continued from prior page]	Am't of tax on the whole tract at the legal rate	Explanation of alterations during the preceeding year, especially from whom transferred	Identification

[No Wrights listed]

1740(062411)

1848 LAND TAX LIST

MONTGOMERY COUNTY, VIRGINIA

Appendix: Montgomery County, Virginia, 1848 Land Tax List:

Davis M. Bennett District:

Name of Owner	Residence	Estate, whether held in fee sim- ple, for life, &c	No. of Acres	Description of the land as to watercourses, moun- tains and contiguous tracts	Distance and bearing from the courthouse	Value of land per acre includ- ing buildings	Sum added to the land on account of buildings	Total value of the land and buildings
John Wright			60		16 N	.25		37.50

Appendix: Montgomery County, Virginia, 1848 Land Tax List:

Davis M. Bennett District:

Name of Owner [Continued from prior page]	Am't of tax on the whole tract, at the legal rate	Explanation of alterations during the preceding year, especially from whom transferred	Identification
John Wright	.60	Deed from Joseph Wright 1847	John B. Wright, son of 1856 Joseph Wright of Roanoke County, grandson of John Wright (Montgomery County), great grandson of 1815 Joseph Wright of Bedford County, and great great grandson of 1763 Thomas Wright of Bedford County

Appendix: Montgomery County, Virginia, 1848 Land Tax List:

Waddy G. Currin District:

Name of Owner	Residence	Estate, whether held in fee sim- ple, for life, &c	No. of Acres	Description of the land as to watercourses, moun- tains and contiguous tracts	Distance and bearing from the courthouse	Value of land per acre includ- ing buildings	Sum added to the land on account of buildings	Total value of the land and buildings
Amos Wright			49	Waters Elliots Creek	4 S	3.00		147.00
"			145			5.00		725.00

Appendix: Montgomery County, Virginia, 1848 Land Tax List:

Waddy G. Currin District:

Name of Owner [Continued from prior page]	Am't of tax on the whole tract, at the legal rate	Explanation of alterations during the preceding year, especially from whom transferred	Identification
Amos Wright	.15		Amos Wright, son of Sarah Wright and grandson of 1826 Joseph Wright of Augusta County
"	.73		

Appendix: Montgomery County, Virginia, 1848 Land Tax List:

Waddy G. Currin District:

Name of Owner	Residence	Estate whether held in fee simple, for life, &c	Number of each lot in the Town	Name of Town	Value of buildings	Value of lots including buildings	Yearly rent of lots
Daniel Wright	Berkley		½ 23 & 24			100	
"			10			40	

Appendix: Montgomery County, Virginia, 1848 Land Tax List:

Waddy G. Currin District:

Name of Owner [Continued from prior page]	Am't of tax on lots, at the legal rate	Explanation of alterations during the preceding year	Identification
Daniel Wright	.10		
"	.04		

1740(062411)

1849 LAND TAX LIST

MONTGOMERY COUNTY, VIRGINIA

Appendix: Montgomery County, Virginia, 1849 Land Tax List:

Waddy G. Curren District:

Name of Owner	Residence	Estate, whether held in fee sim- ple, for life, &c	No. of Acres	Description of the land as to watercourses, moun- tains and contiguous tracts	Distance and bearing from the courthouse	Value of land per acre includ- ing buildings	Sum added to the land on account of buildings	Total value of the land and buildings
Amos Wright	Montgomery	In fee	49	Waters Elliotts Creek	4 S	3.00		147.00
"			145			5.00		725.00

Appendix: Montgomery County, Virginia, 1849 Land Tax List:

Waddy G. Currin District:

Name of Owner [Continued from prior page]	Am't of tax on the whole tract, at the legal rate	Explanation of alterations during the preceding year, especially from whom transferred	Identification
Amos Wright	.15		Amos Wright, son of Sarah Wright and grandson of 1826 Joseph Wright of Augusta County
"	.73		

Appendix: Montgomery County, Virginia, 1849 Land Tax List:

Waddy G. Currin District:

Name of Owner	Residence	Estate whether held in fee simple, for life, &c	Number of each lot in the Town	Name of Town	Value of buildings	Value of lots including buildings	Yearly rent of lots
Daniel Wright	Berkley		½ 23 & 24			100.00	
"			10			40.00	

Appendix: Montgomery County, Virginia, 1849 Land Tax List:

Waddy G. Currin District:

Name of Owner [Continued from prior page]	Am't of tax on lots, at the legal rate	Explanation of alterations during the preceding year	Identification
Daniel Wright	.10		
"	.06		

Appendix: Montgomery County, Virginia, 1849 Land Tax List:

D. M. Bennett District:

Name of Owner	Residence	Estate, whether held in fee sim- ple, for life, &c	No. of Acres	Description of the land as to watercourses, moun- tains and contiguous tracts	Distance and bearing from the courthouse	Value of land per acre includ- ing buildings	Sum added to the land on account of buildings	Total value of the land and buildings

[No Wrights listed]

Appendix: Montgomery County, Virginia, 1849 Land Tax List:

D. M. Bennett District:

Name of Owner [Continued from prior page]	Am't of tax on the whole tract, at the legal rate	Explanation of alterations during the preceding year, especially from whom transferred	Identification

[No Wrights listed]

1740(062411)

1850 LAND TAX LIST

MONTGOMERY COUNTY, VIRGINIA

Appendix: Montgomery County, Virginia, 1850 Land Tax List:

Waddy G. Currin District:

Name of Owner	Residence	Estate, whether held in fee simple, for life, &c	No. of Acres	Description of the land as to watercourses, mountains and contiguous tracts	Distance and bearing from the courthouse	Value of land per acre including buildings	Sum added to the land on account of buildings	Total value of the land and buildings
Amos Wright	Montgomery	In fee	49	Waters Elliotts Creek	4 S	3.00		147.00
"			145			5.00		725.00

Appendix: Montgomery County, Virginia, 1850 Land Tax List:

Waddy G. Currin District:

Name of Owner [Continued from prior page]	Am't of tax on the whole tract, at the legal rate	Explanation of alterations during the preceding year, especially from whom transferred	Identification
Amos Wright	.15		Amos Wright, son of Sarah Wright and grandson of 1826 Joseph Wright of Augusta County
"	.73		

Appendix: Montgomery County, Virginia, 1850 Land Tax List:

Waddy G. Currin District:

Name of Owner	Residence	Estate whether held in fee sim- ple, for life, &c	Number of each lot in the Town	Name of Town	Value of buildings	Value of lots includ- ing buildings	Yearly rent of lots
Daniel Wright	Berkley		½ 23 & 24			100.00	
"			40			40.00	

Appendix: Montgomery County, Virginia, 1850 Land Tax List:

Waddy G. Currin District:

Name of Owner [Continued from prior page]	Am't of tax on lots, at the legal rate	Explanation of alterations during the preceding year	Identification
Daniel Wright	.10		
"	.04		

Appendix: Montgomery County, Virginia, 1850 Land Tax List:

D. M. Bennett District:

Name of Owner	Residence	Estate, whether held in fee simple, for life, &c	No. of Acres	Description of the land as to watercourses, mountains and contiguous tracts	Distance and bearing from the courthouse	Value of land per acre including buildings	Sum added to the land on account of buildings	Total value of the land and buildings
[No Wrights listed]								

Appendix: Montgomery County, Virginia, 1850 Land Tax List:

D. M. Bennett District:

Name of Owner [Continued from prior page]	Am't of tax on the whole tract, at the legal rate	Explanation of alterations during the preceding year, especially from whom transferred	Identification

[No Wrights listed]

INDEX

WRIGHT FAMILY

DEATH RECORDS

1853 TO 1896

MONTGOMERY COUNTY, VIRGINIA

Revised as of June 30, 2011

This document is an appendix to a larger work titled Sorting Some Of The Wrights Of Southern Virginia. The work is divided into parts for each family of Wrights that has been researched. Each part is divided into two sections; the first section is text discussing the family and the evidence supporting the relationships and the second section is a descendants chart summarizing the relationships and information known about each individual.

The appendices to the work (of which this document is one) present source records for persons named Wright by county and by type of record with the identification of the person named and their Wright ancestors to the extent known.

The source for the records listed in this appendix is the following:

1) Montgomery County, Virginia, Death Records, available from the Commonwealth of Virginia, Department of Health, Division of Vital Records, P.O. Box 1000, Richmond, Virginia 23208-1000.

The identification of a person or their ancestor by year and county indicates their year of death and county of residence at death. For example, "1763 Thomas Wright of Bedford County" indicates that this was the Thomas Wright who died in 1763 in Bedford County. If no state is listed after the county, the state is Virginia; counties in states other than Virginia will have a state listed after the county, as in "1876 William S. Wright of Highland County, Ohio".

A parenthetical after the name indicates an identification of the person when a place of death is not yet known, as in "John Wright (Goochland County Carpenter)". A county in parentheses after the name indicates the county with which that person was most identified when no evidence of the place of death has yet been found, as in "Grief Wright (Bedford County)".

All or portions of the text and descendants charts for each Wright family identified are available from the author:

Robert N. Grant
15 Campo Bello Court   (H) 650-854-0895
Menlo Park, California 94025   (O) 650-614-3800

This is a work in progress and I would be most interested in receiving additional information about any of the persons identified in these records in order to correct any errors or expand on the information given.

Appendix: Amherst County, Virginia, Death Records

Book/Page	Date	Decedent	Information	Identification
	1871/09/06	E L Wright	Place: Alleghany Township, Montgomery Co Race: White Sex: Female Cause: Consumption Age: 36 Parents: Birthplace: Occupation: Consort: Alsup Wright Informant: Relationship: Husband	Elizabeth L. (Martin) Wright, wife of Alsup or Alsop Wright, a son of Grief Wright (Bedford County)
	1882/06/15	Hamit Wright	Place: Auburn Dist Montgomery Co Va Race: Colored Sex: Female Cause: Consumption Age: 17 Parents: Allen & Nancy Wright Birthplace: Montgomery Co Va Occupation: Status: Single Informant: Stephen Childress Relationship: Neighbor	Hamit or Harriet Wright, daughter of Allen Wright
	1882/07/13	Ephriam Wright	Place:Auburn Dist Montgomery Co Va Race: Colored Sex: Male Cause: not known Age: 3 mos Parents: Allen & Nancy Wright Birthplace: Montgomery Co Va Occupation: Status: Single Informant: Stephen Childress Relationship: Neighbor	1882 Ephraim Wright of Montgomery County, son of Allen Wright

Book/Page	Date	Decedent	Information	Identification
	1883/11/09	Thomas Wright	Place: Montgomery Co Va Race: Colored Sex: Male Cause: Scrofula Age: 2 Parents: Ferd & Eliza Wright Birthplace: Montgomery Co Va Occupation: none Status: single Informant: F Wright Relationship: Father	1883 Thomas Wright of Montgomery County, son of Ferdinand Wright and grandson of George Wright
	1892/11/24	L. A Wright	Place: Montomery Co Race: Colored Sex: Female Cause: Consumption Age: 25 Parents: unknown Birthplace: Montgomery Co Occupation: farmer Status: Informant: Relationship: friend	

INDEX

0363(063011)

4.

WRIGHT FAMILY

PROBATE RECORDS

1776 TO 1902

MONTGOMERY COUNTY, VIRGINIA

Revised as of June 30, 2011

This document is an appendix to a larger work titled Sorting Some Of The Wrights Of Southern Virginia. The work is divided into parts for each family of Wrights that has been researched. Each part is divided into two sections; the first section is text discussing the family and the evidence supporting the relationships and the second section is a descendants chart summarizing the relationships and information known about each individual.

The appendices to the work (of which this document is one) present source records for persons named Wright by county and by type of record with the identification of the person named and their Wright ancestors to the extent known.

The sources for the records listed in this appendix are the following:

1) Montgomery County Virginia, General Index to Wills and Wills, microfilms #_____, Genealogical Society of the Church of Jesus Christ of the Latter Day Saints.

2) Annals of Southwest Virginia, 1769-1800, by Lewis Preston Summers, Genealogical Publishing Co., Inc., Baltimore, Maryland, 1970.

3) Early Adventurers On The Western Waters, Vols. 1, 2, and 3 by Mary B. Kegley and F. B. Kegley, Green Publishers, Inc., Orange, Virginia, 1980, 1982, and 1993.

4) Montgomery County, Va Will Book 1 1786-1809, by James L. Douthat, Mountain Press, P.O. Box 400, Signal Mountain, Tennessee 37377-0400, 1986.

The identification of a person or their ancestor by year and county indicates their year of death and county of residence at death. For example, "1763 Thomas Wright of Bedford County" indicates that this was the Thomas Wright who died in 1763 in Bedford County. If no state is listed after the county, the state is Virginia; counties in states other than Virginia will have a state listed after the county, as in "1876 William S. Wright of Highland County, Ohio".

A parenthetical after the name indicates an identification of the person when a place of death is not yet known, as in "John Wright (Goochland County Carpenter)". A county in parentheses after the name indicates the county with which that person was most identified when no evidence of the place of death has yet been found, as in "Grief Wright (Bedford County)".

All or portions of the text and descendants charts for each Wright family identified are available from the author:

Robert N. Grant
15 Campo Bello Court   (H) 650-854-0895
Menlo Park, California 94025   (O) 650-614-3800

This is a work in progress and I would be most interested in receiving additional information about any of the persons identified in these records in order to correct any errors or expand on the information given.

Appendix: Montgomery County, Virginia, Probate Records:

Book/Page		Date	Name	Instrument	Identification
02	446	1816/09/18	Reed Wright	Manumission of Slave	
03	239	1820/09/25	Richard Wright	Deed of Trust	
08	160	1850/12/02	Sarah Wright	Will	Sarah Wright, daughter of 1826 Joseph Wright of Augusta County
08	166	1851/01/00	Sarah Wright	Appraisement	Sarah Wright, daughter of 1826 Joseph Wright of Augusta County
08	274	1851/10/00	Sarah Wright	Settlement	Sarah Wright, daughter of 1826 Joseph Wright of Augusta County
09	104	1857/04/06	Daniel Wright	Power of Atty	Daniel Wright, son of Harry Wright
09	202	1858/07/12	John H. Wright	Deed of Trust	John H. Wright, son of 1841 Price Wright of Bedford County, grandson of 1835 Benjamin Wright of Bedford County, great grandson of 1814 John Wright of Bedford County, and great great grandson of John Wright (Goochland County Carpenter)
12	504	1902/01/00	John M. Wright	Will	1902 John M. Wright of Montgomery County, son of James A. Wright (Floyd County), grandson of Joseph Wright (Augusta County), and great grandson of 1826 Joseph Wright of Augusta County

Heritage Books by Robert N. Grant

Identifying the Wrights in the Goochland County, Virginia Tithe Lists, 1732–84

The Identification of 1792 John Wright of Fauquier County, Virginia, as Not the Son of 1792/30 John Wright of Stafford County, Virginia

The Identification of 1809 William Wright of Franklin County, Virginia, as the Son of 1792 John Wright of Fauquier County, Virginia, and Elizabeth (Bronaugh) (Darnall) Wright

Wright Family Birth, Marriage, and Personal Property Tax Records, Montgomery County, Virginia

Wright Family Birth Records (1853–1896) and Marriage Records (1788–1915): Franklin County, Virginia, 1853–1896

Wright Family Birth Records, 1853–1896; Marriage Records, 1761–1900; Census Records, 1810–1900, in Amherst County, Virginia

*Wright Family Birth Records, 1853–1896; Marriage Records, 1808–1910; Census Records, 1810–1900; Patent Deeds and Land Grants;
Deed Records, 1808–1910; Death Records, 1853–1896; Probate Records, 1808–1900, in Nelson County, Virginia*

*Wright Family Birth Records, 1853–1896; Marriage Records, 1777–1918; Census Records, 1810–1900; Deed Records, 1777–1902;
Death Records, 1853–1896; Cemetery Records, and Probate Records, 1777–1909; in Rockbridge County, Virginia*

Wright Family Birth Records (1853–1896) and Marriage Records (1782–1900): Campbell County, Virginia

Wright Family Birth Records, Marriage Records, and Personal Property Tax Lists: Appomattox County, Virginia

Wright Family Census, Land Grants, Land Tax, Deed, Death, and Probate Records, Montgomery County, Virginia

Wright Family Census Records, Deed Records, Land Tax Lists, Death Records and Probate Records: Appomattox County, Virginia

Wright Family Census Records: Bedford County, Virginia, 1810–1900

Wright Family Census Records: Campbell County, Virginia, 1810–1900

Wright Family Census Records: Franklin County, Virginia, 1810–1900

Wright Family Death Records (1853–1920), Cemetery Records by Cemetery, and Probate Records (1782–1900): Campbell County, Virginia

Wright Family Death Records (1854–1920), Cemetery Records by Cemetery, and Probate Records (1785–1928): Franklin County, Virginia

Wright Family Death, Cemetery and Probate Records: Bedford County, Virginia

Wright Family Deed Records (1782–1900) and Land Tax List (1782–1850): Campbell County, Virginia

Wright Family Land Grants (1785–1900) and Deed Records (1785–1897): Franklin County, Virginia

Wright Family Land Grants, Deed Records, Land Tax List, Death Records, Probate Records: Prince Edward County, Virginia

Wright Family Land Records: Bedford County, Virginia

Wright Family Land Tax Lists: Franklin County, Virginia, 1786–1860

Wright Family Land Tax Lists: Rockbridge County, Virginia, 1782–1850

Wright Family Land Tax Records: Amherst County, Virginia, 1782–1850

Wright Family Land Tax Records: Nelson County, Virginia, 1809–1850

*Wright Family Patent Deeds and Land Grants, 1761–1900, Deed Records, 1761–1903; Chancery Court Files, 1804–1900;
Death Records, 1853–1920; Cemetery Records by Cemetery; and Probate Records, 1761–1900, in Amherst County, Virginia*

Wright Family Personal Property Tax Lists: Amherst County, Virginia, 1782–1850

Wright Family Personal Property Tax Lists: Campbell County, Virginia, 1785–1850

Wright Family Personal Property Tax Lists: Franklin County, Virginia, 1786–1850

Wright Family Personal Property Tax Lists: Nelson County, Virginia, 1809–1850

Wright Family Personal Property Tax Lists: Rockbridge County, Virginia, 1782–1850

Wright Family Personal Property Tax Records for Bedford County, Virginia, 1782 to 1850

Wright Family Records: Births in Bedford County, Virginia

Wright Family Records: Land Tax List, Bedford County, Virginia, 1782–1850

Wright Family Records: Lynchburg, Virginia Birth Records (1853–1896), Marriage Records (1805–1900), Marriage Notices (1794–1880), Census Records (1900), Deed Records (1805–1900), Death Records (1853–1896), Probate Records (1805–1900)

Wright Family Records: Marriages in Bedford County, Virginia

Wright Family Records: Prince Edward County, Virginia Birth Records, Marriage Records, Election Polls, and Tithe List, Personal Property Tax List, Census

www.ingramcontent.com/pod-product-compliance
Lightning Source LLC
Chambersburg PA
CBHW080233270326
41926CB00020B/4215